BREAD, BRICKS, AND BELIEF

Kumarian Press Books for a World that Works

Bread, Bricks, and Belief:
Communities In Charge of Their Future
Mary Lean

GAZA: Legacy of Occupation—A Photographer's Journey
Dick Doughty and Mohammed El Aydi

When Corporations Rule the World
David C. Korten

HIV & AIDS:
The Global Inter-Connection
Elizabeth Reid, editor

All Her Paths Are Peace:
Women Pioneers in Peacemaking
Michael Henderson

The Human Farm:
A Tale of Changing Lives and Changing Lands
Katie Smith

Summer in the Balkans:
Laughter and Tears after Communism
Randall Baker

Voices from the Amazon
Binka Le Breton

BREAD, BRICKS, AND BELIEF

Communities In Charge of Their Future

Mary Lean

Kumarian Press

Kumarian Press Books for a World that Works

Bread, Bricks, and Belief: Communities In Charge of Their Future Published 1995 in the United States of America by
Kumarian Press, Inc.
630 Oakwood Avenue, Suite 119
West Hartford, Connecticut 06110-1529 USA

Production supervised by Jenna Dixon
Copyedited by Linda Faillace   *Proofread by Michele Brown*
Text designed by Jenna Dixon   *Typeset by Ultragraphics*
Index prepared by Mary Neumann

Printed in the United States of America on recycled acid-free paper by
Thomson-Shore, Inc. Text printed with soy-based ink.

Library of Congress Cataloging-in-Publication Data
Lean, Mary.
    Bread, bricks, and belief : communities in charge of their future / Mary Lean.
        p.   cm. — (Kumarian Press books for a world that works)
    Includes bibliographic references and index.
    ISBN 1-56549-046-0 (pbk. : alk. paper)
    1. Community development—Case studies. 2. Sustainable development—
Case studies. I. Title. II. Series.
HN49.C6L43   1995
307.1'4—dc20   95-14670

04 03 02 01 00 99 98 97 96 95 10 9 8 7 6 5 4 3 2 1   1st Printing 1995

Contents

Preface

This book began to germinate ten years ago, in a temple in a remote village in the Indian state of Maharashtra.

I arrived in India in November 1984 to find the country still reeling from the intercommunal violence sparked by Indira Gandhi's assassination a few weeks before. Charis Waddy, a British scholar who had devoted her life to building bridges with Islam, had invited me to accompany her on a speaking tour. I had just begun writing on environment and development and so, as well as assisting Dr. Waddy, I was eager to learn more about these issues in India.

While we were in Delhi, I seized the chance to visit the environmentalist N. D. Jayal, then an adviser to India's planning commission and now natural heritage director of the Indian National Trust for Art and Cultural Heritage. Two months before, speaking to the general assembly of the International Union for the Conservation of Nature and Natural Resources (IUCN), he had warned that deforestation was destroying India's water resources. In Maharashtra, for instance, 22,000 villages had seen their water supplies dry up. He told me that if I wrote only one story as a result of my visit to India, it should be about Ralegan Siddhi, a drought-prone village near Pune that had undergone a remarkable transformation. Its experience made him believe that there was hope for India yet.

It was surprisingly easy to get there. Friends in Pune arranged for me to join a busload of farmers from another part of Maharashtra, organized by a local company as part of its rural development outreach. Our hosts ushered us into the temple. As the sparrows flew in and out, tugging at the brightly colored paper decorations and swinging on the bells, the villagers told us how Ralegan Siddhi had come back from the dead.

Ten years before, the village had been crippled by drought. Now it was thriving, thanks to the efforts of its inhabitants. They showed us the wells they had dug, the houses and schools they had built, the windmill and biogas plants they had erected, the trees they had planted, the flourishing crops. And they insisted that none of these achievements could have happened without the deep spiritual change that had empowered them to work together. The temple was not just their meeting place; it was the powerhouse of the village's development.

My visit to Ralegan Siddhi—which I describe in greater detail in Chapter 1—brought together two areas of my life: my concern for sustainable development, which meets the needs of present generations without jeopardizing future ones, and my conviction that what happens inside people affects what happens around them. This theme is central to my work with Moral Re-Armament (MRA), an international program that makes the link between inner motivation, social change, and conflict resolution. It encourages people to examine their own lives and to seek inspiration from God as a first step in addressing the problems they see around them.

I returned home and wrote the story, which was syndicated around the world by Earthscan. Two years later, some friends and I launched the international magazine *For a Change*, with a mission to seek out similar stories of the link between faith and action.

This book is a product of that search, which has taken me and my colleagues to many countries. It tells the stories of communities on five continents and from several faiths that have taken charge of their own destinies. It does not pretend to be comprehensive. The fact that there are no examples from Africa, for instance, does not mean that none exist, merely that they have not come my way. The fact that there are more examples from Christianity than from other religions, and that several of the people featured have links with MRA, reflects my own sources as a Christian and an MRA worker. I hope that this book will encourage others to explore the catalytic role of faith in community development and to write from their own traditions.

I interviewed many of those whose stories I tell in their home communities or at international conferences. In some cases, I had to rely on the research of others; I drew throughout on the knowledge and experience of observers close to the situations described. These people are acknowledged at the end of the relevant chapters.

I would like to thank all those who read drafts of the book and contributed their thoughts and criticism: my brother Geoffrey Lean, Wim Aspeslagh, Anne Hamlin, Erika Hetzner, Elizabeth Locke, and Hugh Nowell. Thanks too to Peter Rundell and Donatus da Silva for their advice; to all at Kumarian Press for their painstaking work and encouragement, particularly Ian Mayo-Smith, Krishna Sondhi, and Trish Reynolds; to my colleagues at *For a Change*—Kenneth Noble, Edward Peters, Michael Smith, Choice Okoro, Michelle Hemenway, and Alan Channer—for their support and tolerance; and to my mother, sister-in-law, and friends.

While I was working on this book, my father, the author Garth Lean, died. He taught me how to write and, more important still, how to delete. He wrote his own books to challenge what he described as the "helplessness syndrome": the illusion "that the individual is helpless, unable to do anything to alter events." He believed deeply that one could be an agent of change if one was ready to start in one's own life, and he spent many hours helping individuals do this. This book is dedicated to him, in love and gratitude.

CHAPTER 1

A Forgotten Factor

Twenty years ago, the village of Ralegan Siddhi, forty-five miles northeast of the Indian city of Pune, was dying of thirst.[1] With the rains uncertain at the best of times and with frequent droughts, even its most prosperous farmers barely maintained subsistence level. Villagers were talking of migrating to Pune and Bombay, where thousands of refugees from poor villages sleep on the pavements every night.

Today, nobody in Ralegan Siddhi goes hungry, and the villagers have surpluses to sell. When the worst drought in forty years hit the area in the late 1980s, they grew fodder for their neighbors' starving cattle.

Ralegan Siddhi owes its transformation to a charismatic leader, sound environmental principles, and, according to its inhabitants, their own moral and spiritual rebirth. At the hub of its renaissance stands the Hindu temple, with its green and terra-cotta posts, its shrines, and its communal television set. It serves as headquarters, meeting place, medical dispensary, warehouse, and source of inspiration.

The events leading to the village's recovery began in 1965, when an Indian army truck was caught in an ambush during the India-Pakistan War. All its passengers were killed or maimed except for the twenty-three-year-old driver, who came from Ralegan Siddhi. "Anna" (Brother) Hazare, as he is now universally called, had been going through a period of spiritual search and had once been so depressed by the disparities in society and the apparent pointlessness of existence that he had contemplated suicide. His narrow escape convinced him that God wanted him to serve his community.

Ten years later he returned to Ralegan Siddhi and set up home in the temple, adopting a life of celibacy and service. He had no definite plans, he told me, but one thing led to another. In the process, he discovered and made full use of the resources offered by governmental and other agencies.

The first step was to raise morale in a community where the only thriving professions were bootlegging and moneylending. There were forty illegal distilleries for a population of 1,500, and drunken disputes and crimes were frequent, undermining opportunities for common action. Only a fifth of the villagers were able to grow enough food to feed themselves.

Hazare started out with a small youth group. "Initially the response was very slow," he says. To grab the villagers' attention, he staged a seven-day religious recitation marathon, and this gave rise to a decision to extend the temple. The villagers decided to finance this work by selling the fruit from trees that grew on the borders between properties, a frequent source of disputes.

The hard drinkers began to come to the temple to take the pledge, and the stills closed down. Later the villagers bought up the shops' cigarette stocks and burnt them. "Addiction was the cause of all our troubles," Hazare explains. "Without prohibition, we could make no progress."

Water was the villagers' top priority. Like some 7,000 other villages in the state, Ralegan Siddhi relied on the unpredictable rains to water its crops. Its problem was how to store the rain that fell during the monsoon rather than letting it run away in seasonal rivers and streams.

Drawing on information garnered by Hazare, the villagers began by building small dams along the course of the river, which is dry for most of the year, to catch the monsoon rain. They also took steps to increase the soil's capacity to retain moisture and to prevent erosion. They planted thousands of trees, choosing species that would nourish the earth and provide fodder, fruit, firewood, and timber. They sowed a mixture of crops in their fields to deter pests and feed the soil, and they used organic

Anna Hazare of Ralegan Siddhi, a village which came back from the dead

manure, which is both cheaper than chemical fertilizers and more conducive to soil humidity. They installed biogas plants to convert animal and vegetable wastes into methane gas for cooking and slurry for the fields. They built communal latrines to feed the biogas plants.

The community pooled its labor to build a nursery school, where each child planted and was responsible for his or her own tree. The villagers also built a secondary school, saving pupils a thirteen-mile journey. They constructed homes for landless Harijan families, the former "untouchables" of the Hindu caste system, who are still condemned to hovels in most villages. Most of the funds came from government subsidies and bank loans, which were promptly repaid. The villagers also paid their share— 10 percent in the case of the farmers whose land was watered by the lift irrigation schemes.

When I visited Ralegan Siddhi in 1985, the village had been feeding itself for two years. That year, for the first time, there was surplus grain to sell. Incomes had risen, and the villagers maintained that crime and drunkenness had ceased. Health had improved, thanks to better nutrition and sanitation. Their achievement was all the more remarkable in a world where loss of soil fertility robs millions of their livelihoods.

Hazare, who has been decorated by the Indian government, is convinced that the transformation of Ralegan Siddhi began inside the villagers themselves. "The main burden of Hazare's song is human values, moral values, and spirituality," says R. U. Chandrachood, a former director of the Khadi and Cottage Industries Commission. "He believes that unless these values are cherished, no amount of development is going to help."

The experience of Ralegan Siddhi illustrates the central contentions of this book: that development is at its most creative and sustainable when it rises from people at the grassroots; that what happens inside people is a key to what happens around them; and that religious and spiritual experience can play a creative role in this process.

A village in one of the developing countries of the South[2] is a good place to begin a book on community development, for it is there that the world's poorest people live. According to the United Nations Development Program (UNDP), a third of the people of these countries live in "abject poverty," a quarter have no supply of safe drinking water, and a fifth go hungry.[3] Every day, 34,000 small children die as a result of malnutrition and disease.[4] These conditions are worst in the countryside; as a result, some 20 million people flood into the cities every year.[5] There they find new problems: industrial pollution, crime, overcrowding, homelessness, and unemployment.

The poor are the losers in a world whose economic structures are stacked toward the rich and powerful. On a global level, developing countries struggle up a down escalator of debt repayments and falling commodity prices. Within countries, city-based governments concentrate on appeasing the volatile urban masses near their seats of power, often at the expense of country dwellers. In both the developed North and the developing South, there is a yawning gap between rich and poor. The poorest 40 percent of Americans receive only 16 percent of the total national income, whereas the poorest 40 percent of Brazilians receive just 7 percent.[6]

Both global and national economies need reform, and so do our concepts of development. Traditional views of development have overemphasized economics and ignored the true aspirations of the poor, maintains Robert Chambers of the Institute of Development Studies at the University of Sussex.[7] He quotes researchers who have found that poor people measure progress and well-being in terms not just of income but of health, security, power, and self-respect. "What [the poor] value and choose often differs from what outsider professionals expect," he concludes. The UNDP's 1994 *Human Development Report* appealed for "a new development paradigm" that is "pro-people, pro-jobs and pro-nature" and enables poor communities to "design and participate in the processes and events that shape their lives."

Development of this sort cannot be dispensed from above. "For development to help the poor, it must put them first not only as intended beneficiaries but as active participants, advisers and leaders," maintains Washington's Worldwatch Institute. "True development does not simply provide for the needy, it enables them to provide for themselves."[8] It is as needed in the violent and socially dysfunctional inner cities of the North as it is in the South.

All over the world, there is evidence that when local people come together they can achieve amazing things. Hundreds of thousands of self-help community groups have sprung up over the last few decades: from tricycle couriers in the Dominican Republic to women planting trees in Kenya; from mothers fighting the drug trade in northeastern India to housing cooperatives in the United States. They are as varied in their composition as they are in their purposes. Alan Durning, writing for the Worldwatch Institute, describes them as the "ragtag front line" in the fight against poverty and environmental destruction.[9]

"For those who live on the brink of starvation, generations of misfortune and injustice have bred an often overwhelming fatalism," writes Durning. "Life experience counsels them that change is impossible and that those who offer to help have ulterior motives."[10] In addition, many communities are deeply divided by class, personality conflicts, factional friction, and squabbles.

What does it take to break the bonds of inertia and mistrust? Often a crisis acts as a catalyst: a natural threat, such as soil erosion or flooding, or a human one, such as an eviction attempt. Frequently, an individual takes the lead. Sometimes it is someone from outside, but the most effective leader is a local person—like Anna Hazare in Ralegan Siddhi—who understands the community's personalities, customs, beliefs, and problems and is known by the people.

Getting people to work together is not just a practical issue but also a spiritual one, in the sense that it concerns motivation, attitudes, and relationships—what Sri Lankan thinker and journalist Varindra Tarzie Vittachi called the "in-vironment."[11] Successful community action depends on learning to listen to one another, to resolve conflicts, and to overcome barriers of fear and suspicion. And these qualities are the fruit of inner growth.

This spiritual dimension has often been the forgotten factor in community development. Western experts, blinkered by their own secular worldview, tend to overlook the spirituality of the poor—and its potential for empowerment.

Laurence Taylor, director of development studies at the Selly Oak Colleges in Britain, tells the story of a group of Norwegian bureaucrats deputed to evaluate a project in Zimbabwe. When the community meeting they attended opened with a prayer, they objected: their money should not be used to fund prayer meetings. Their hosts were amazed. "We open all our meetings with prayer," they said. "Don't you?"

"Western society generally has marginalized religion," comments Taylor. "Our values are secular and financial. But the attitudes of most people in the world are highly underwritten by spiritual attitudes. Religion is part of their holistic view of life. They feel we have lost something."

The Enlightenment of the eighteenth century brought to the West a reliance on reason and proof, in contrast to the often superstitious beliefs of previous centuries. It brokered a divorce between the "objective" world of the sciences and technology and the "subjective" world of feelings and faith. Many philosophers wrote religion off as "dogmatic and superstitious, irrational and not empirically grounded, socially escapist and in collusion with oppressive regimes, an expression of psychological immaturity or existentially crippling."[12]

In Western societies, faith became a private, personal matter, with little relation to the working world. "Our society has fashioned itself around this 'core idea' that the purpose of life is to produce, consume and acquire," writes Christopher Titmuss, a British Buddhist. "Religious beliefs are just an appendix, providing the consolation of eternal life rather than extinction."[13]

On both national and global levels, religious faith is strong at the grassroots and weak among the educated elite. This can create a gulf of misunderstanding between the experts and those they seek to serve. As development thought edges away from top-down prescriptions toward heeding the poor as the true experts on poverty, it must take on a fundamental aspect of their mind-set—their awareness of the spiritual dimension.

Nearly half of the world's population belongs to one of the world's four largest religions, and if the 1.2 billion people in officially atheist China are excluded, the proportion rises. In most developing countries, faith is almost universal, at least nominally. Over 80 percent of Indians are Hindu, and another 10 percent are Muslim; over 80 percent of Bangladeshis and Indonesians and 96 percent of Pakistanis are Muslim; 95 percent of Thais and 88 percent of Cambodians are Buddhist. Nearly half of the people in Africa's most populous nation, Nigeria, are Muslim; over a third are Christian, and over a tenth belong to indigenous faiths. Over 130 million Brazilians are Catholics.[14]

In these countries, faith is a fundamental cultural fact. "The worldview of the vast majority of poor people in the Third World is essentially religious," says Jeff Thindwa, a Malawian who is director of relief and development for World Vision, UK. "It is unfortunate that we are operating in an environment where the spiritual and religious are not viewed as politically correct. But not to engage with the poor in ways that relate to their spirituality is to be politically incorrect with them. Development workers who have no ear for the spirituality of the poor are in danger of becoming irrelevant in the long term."

The experience of Ralegan Siddhi demonstrates two ways in which the spiritual dimension can contribute to community action. First, religion—a formal and established system of belief—can be a resource. In using the temple as a rallying point, Hazare drew on his community's Hindu faith to inspire and legitimize action. He launched his work with a religious event and sustained it with religious practices: wells and buildings were dedicated to Hindu saints, and loudspeakers roused the villagers every morning for religious exhortations and devotions. In so doing, he established development work as not just a social necessity but a religious duty.

Hazare's experience is not unique. In 1980, Balbir Mathur returned to India after over twenty years in business in the United States, determined to devote the rest of his life to tree planting in the villages. His first attempts to interest people failed: not even his mother would accept a sapling. Then he struck on the idea of asking a local Hindu holy man to bless the saplings, and suddenly everyone wanted one.

By 1989, his organization, Trees for Life, was planting 700,000 trees a year. "Wherever possible, we distribute trees as *prasadam* [spiritual blessing], whether from temples, *gurdwaras* [Sikh temples], or mosques—it doesn't matter," says Mathur. "Westerners don't understand this, but that doesn't make any difference—the religious or spiritual centering of the tree is very important." Reporting the story, Ranchor Prime comments, "Planting trees had to be more than a mere good deed, it had to be a transcendental action, one that appealed to the deep-seated spiritual conscience of the Indian people."[15]

In Cambodia, a country struggling back to normality after years of horror and holocaust, Buddhist monasteries provide a focus for community efforts. Some run "rice banks" from which farmers can draw in lean times and pay back at harvest. The fact that these banks are within the monastery walls puts a spiritual obligation on borrowers to repay their loans.

Even when religious customs obstruct development, change may come more easily from a religious than a secular source. The Buddhist Tamang community in Bans Kharka, a village in the mountains of Nepal, had a tradition of building cairns on the hilltops in memory of their dead. Each death meant clearing a patch of forest for a cairn, and as the years went on, firewood and fodder began to run out.

The community's leader, Laxman Dong, enlisted the local priests to help convince the villagers that they should build a monastery in which to hold their rituals as an alternative to hill-top sites, and that they should cremate the bodies in fuel-efficient crematoria. The cairns were dismantled, and the stones were used to build the monastery. Villagers were required to plant five trees as a tax before they could register births, marriages, or deaths. Today, forty years later, there are so many trees around the village that the tax has been cut to one tree.

Dong convinced the community that "building a drinking water scheme is as much an act of *dharma* [virtuous action] as prayers." The community now has drinking water, sanitation, a health center, irrigated fields, and grain to sell to outsiders. Other villages are following its example, in a country where 123,500 acres of forest are cleared every year and 13 million people depend on wood for fuel.[16]

In the Christian world, the Christian Base Communities (CBCs) linked to the Catholic Church in Latin America provide one of the best illustrations of the rallying power of religion at the grassroots. CBCs bring people together to look at their lives in the light of their faith and at their faith in the light of their lives. They draw on the teaching of Paulo Freire, who coined the word "conscientization" to describe a process through which people become critically aware of their situation, find the confidence to do something about it and the conscientiousness to do it well, and learn to act together. "Conscientization can become a powerful process for transforming a group of frightened or fatalistic peasants or favela-dwellers into a cohesive force for social justice," comments Charles Elliott, former head of Christian Aid.[17]

A typical CBC has between twenty and fifty members and meets for worship, Bible study, mutual support, and action. The CBC of São José, on the edge of São Paulo, Brazil, was one of seventeen in its parish in 1988. Originally started by parents who wanted to provide religious education for their children, it moved on to negotiating legal titles for the plots on which the community was squatting and obtaining water, sewerage, streetlights, and street paving.[18] There are thought to be between 80,000 and 100,000 such groups in Brazil and over 200,000 in Latin America as a whole. The movement has also been influential in the Philippines, where CBCs on the island of Mindanao led a successful campaign to ban logging of the forests in the late 1980s.[19]

These examples demonstrate that religion can be a powerful resource in development. Of course, this is not always the case. Religion can also be an opiate, particularly when it reinforces fatalism. It can be a source of division, as when Christian denominations use development work as a weapon in the competition for adherents. Treasured customs or rigid dogmas may obstruct progress. But when these pitfalls are avoided, development that is grounded in faith has two outstanding advantages. It builds on a community's deepest sense of identity and belonging, and it carries within it the seeds of individual empowerment.

The second theme raised by the example of Ralegan Siddhi is the creative force of inner change. Hazare's understanding of development embraced not only material circumstances but also the personal growth and transformation of those involved. He saw that if the villagers could overcome their alcohol problem, they would find it easier to work together. Drawing on their common belief system, he encouraged drinkers to take the pledge in the temple: "taking a vow in the temple gives the person the strength to keep it."

All such inner change is spiritual in the most basic sense of the word—relating to the nonmaterial dimension—whatever its links to formal religion. Several activists highlighted in this book trace their inspiration to Mahatma Gandhi's nonsectarian approach and to his belief that activists must embody the change they want to see in the world. Others found inner liberation through Alcoholics Anonymous and the recovery movement, which take a spiritual but nonreligious approach. Others still have been influenced by Moral Re-Armament (MRA), an international network of people of all faiths that encourages people to make real in their own lives the changes they want to see in society.

A spiritual experience can transform an individual's life and enable him or her to become an agent of change. Hazare's escape from death was a "Damascus Road" experience, a personal encounter with the ultimate reality beyond material existence, which he perceived as God. It set his life on a new path and spurred him into action in his village. An encounter of this sort liberates and changes an individual and impacts his or her behavior and relationships.

A meeting in New Delhi in October 1993, sponsored by the World Evangelical Fellowship, examined this factor from a Christian perspective and concluded that spiritual rebirth

> gives poor people faith, patience and courage to endure physical and moral suffering, and the confidence that God will provide for their basic human needs. It also liberates people to stand with others in resisting the oppression they suffer. . . . People are encouraged to change their lives, to seek to change the lives of their families and neighbors, and to create families, disciples and wealth.[20]

This is the opposite of offering relief and development as a reward for conversion; rather, it urges the importance of deep spiritual change as a means to effective action.

Those meeting in New Delhi saw inner change in Christian terms, but, as Hazare demonstrates, it is not a solely Christian phenomenon. In the 1960s, a group of young men in a Harijan colony in Delhi set up an evening school for local children and began to meet daily to plan how to improve things in their community. The spur had been a visit to the colony by an outsider, Rajmohan Gandhi, grandson of the Mahatma. Gandhi had told the young Harijans, "Don't think of yourself as an untouchable but think what you can do for India and the world." He encouraged them to follow the Gandhian practice of listening to the inner voice in their hearts and to put right the things that weighed on their consciences. This helped them find the will and confidence to work for their community. Thirty years later, in spite of relapses over the years, some of them are still at it.[21]

For many of those featured in this book, liberation began in areas that might seem far removed from community needs: their personal lifestyles and habits; their relationships with their spouses, families, and neighbors. To say that people can be empowered when they turn their backs on addiction, dishonesty, and personal rivalries is not the same as blaming the poor for their poverty. If people cease to feel hopeless about themselves, they have a better chance of breaking out of their helplessness when it comes to external circumstances. When they overcome intractable personal problems (or, to use Christian language, "sin"), when they believe that God is on their side and no problem is beyond him, they find that they can do things they never believed possible.

This was true for Lawrence Fearon, an ex-offender who helped set up a multimillion-dollar community center in a depressed area of London (see Chapter 8). He says, "One of the inferiorities that develops is 'I've committed a crime, I wasn't a very good student at school, didn't leave with qualifications—how can I ever begin to do anything?' There had to be a spiritual encounter to overcome that. I couldn't even begin to try with the old self. That spiritual experience conquered the fear and inferiority."

Those who believe that God will sustain and guide them have extra resources on which they can draw when the going gets rough, as it so often does in community work. Laurence Taylor, a Christian, compares it to the transfer lever on a four-wheel-drive vehicle: "People who take seriously the idea of having access to the power of the Holy Spirit can look at these awful quagmires and engage that power. It gives them a confidence to tackle problems that other people wouldn't."

A Vietnamese Buddhist monk, Thich Nhat Hanh, puts it this way: "We see many groups with plenty of goodwill. They agree completely with each other on the analysis of the situation, but when they come to action they fail because they cannot act in harmony. After some time they start fighting with each other and can no longer serve their cause at all. This is because they lack a spiritual dimension to their actions."[22]

"Where community work has had some measure of success, there has always been a seed of something else, some recognition that in the final analysis the physical and material are limited," maintains Selena Tapper, Caribbean representative of the Canadian Universities Services Overseas (CUSO). "Over the years we have found that however much money we pour in, it falls through the hole. This has led some of us to believe that the economic problem is not our biggest problem. We need to give value to something the Caribbean has not lost yet—the spiritual side of life. Development is not just about material well-being."

To overlook the spiritual is to discount one of the most potent factors in development. The examples in this book—from villages and cities in the South and from inner-city communities in the North—attest to the creative energy released when people take spiritual life seriously. This book is a celebration, and an exploration, of its power and versatility.

Notes

Unless otherwise stated, direct quotations are taken from my own interviews with those concerned. Thanks to Col. and Mrs. Rege of Pune, and to Bajaj Auto of Pune, for arranging my visits to Ralegan Siddhi.

1. A more detailed account of Ralegan Siddhi's development can be found in Ganesh Pangare and Vasudha Pangare, *From Poverty to Plenty: The Story of Ralegan Siddhi* (New Delhi: Indian National Trust for Art and Cultural Heritage, 1992).
2. I have chosen to use the terms "South" and "North" to describe the developing, unindustrialized and developed, industrialized worlds, respectively, because they are both concise and unweighted. In this context, developed countries such as New Zealand and Australia are included in the North, in spite of their geographic location.

3. UNDP, *Human Development Report, 1994* (New York/Oxford: Oxford University Press, 1994).
4. UNDP, *Human Development Report, 1993* (New York/Oxford: Oxford University Press, 1993).
5. Herbert Girardet, *The Gaia Atlas of Cities* (London: Gaia Books, 1992).
6. UNDP, *Human Development Report, 1994.*
7. Robert Chambers, "Poverty and Livelihoods: Whose Reality Counts?" (overview paper for the UNDP Stockholm Roundtable on Global Change, July 1994).
8. Alan B. Durning, "Ending Poverty," in *State of the World 1990: Worldwatch Institute Report* (New York: W. W. Norton, 1990), 149.
9. Alan B. Durning, "Mobilizing at the Grassroots," in *State of the World 1989: Worldwatch Institute Report* (New York: W. W. Norton, 1989), 154.
10. Durning, "Mobilizing," 159.
11. Varindra Tarzie Vittachi, open letter to the Media Seminar of the Global Forum of Spiritual and Parliamentary Leaders, Okayama, Japan, April 1993.
12. Donald Rothberg, "The Crisis of Modernity and the Emergence of Socially Engaged Spirituality," *ReVision* (Winter 1993): 107.
13. Christopher Titmuss, *Freedom of the Spirit: More Voices of Hope for a World in Crisis* (London: Green Print, 1991), 1–2.
14. *Philips' International World Atlas* (London: George Philips, 1992).
15. Ranchor Prime, *Hinduism and Ecology* (London: Cassell/World Wide Fund for Nature, 1992), 86, 87.
16. Binod Bhattarai, *Foresting with Faith in Nepal* (UNICEF Feature No. 00041-NEP).
17. Charles Elliott, *Sword and Spirit* (London: BBC Books/Marshall Pickering, 1989), 61.
18. W. E. Hewitt, *Base Christian Communities and Social Change in Brazil* (Lincoln: University of Nebraska Press, 1991).
19. Karl M. Gaspar, *A People's Option: To Struggle for Creation* (Quezon City: Claretian Publications, 1990); Vin McMullen, *Looking at the Philippines Through the Eyes of the Poor* (London: Catholic Fund for Overseas Development, 1992).
20. "The New Delhi Statement," *Evangelical Review of Theology,* April 1994.
21. Kenneth Noble, "Breaking the Bonds of Caste," *For a Change,* May 1988.
22. Martine Batchelor and Kerry Brown, eds., *Buddhism and Ecology* (London: Cassell/World Wide Fund for Nature, 1992), 103.

Part I

Village Voices: The South

Some 2.75 billion people—more than two-thirds of the population of the South—live in villages in developing countries.[1] Among them are the poorest people on earth.

World poverty is a predominantly rural phenomenon. Nearly a quarter of the world's population lives in absolute poverty, unable to meet their own most basic needs.[2] Four-fifths of these people live in rural areas.[3] They see their children die from diseases related to dirty water; they search farther every day for wood for their fires; they struggle to grow crops in soil worn out by overuse and erosion; they go hungry in the rainy season before they can harvest their food; they are at the mercy of natural disasters and rapacious landowners. Their strategies for survival are amazingly versatile, involving whole families in a wide range of ways of finding food, fuel, income, and support. But they have few resources with which to cope with emergencies.[4]

The world's poorest people are landless, powerless, often illiterate, and far from the offices and conference tables where economies are planned. Unlike the urban poor, whose riots can shake the citadels of power, they are silent and easily overlooked by decision makers at home and abroad.

The rural poor of the South lose out in both the global and the national marketplaces. They live in countries whose economies are shackled by debts incurred when interest rates were low, by the falling prices of their commodities sold overseas, and by the trade barriers stacked against their manu-factures.

By the end of the 1980s, developing countries owed nearly half their collective gross national product to Northern banks and governments. The prices of thirty-three of their main exports fell an average of 40 percent between 1980 and 1987. The inter-national cash flow had gone into reverse: by 1988, developing countries were paying the North $50 billion a year more than they had received in aid, loans, and payments.[5]

This imbalance is mirrored within most developing nations, where a rich minority govern a poor majority. Such govern-ments favor the cities at the expense of the villages. They pacify the urban masses with low food prices at the expense of rural farmers. On average, the villagers of the South get less than half their fair share of educational, health, water, and sanitary ser-vices.[6] Thirty-eight percent of the developing world's rural communities go without clean water, and 55 percent without sanitation (as compared with 15 and 25 percent, respectively, of city dwellers).[7] Infant mortality, disease, malnutrition, and illit-eracy all flourish in the countryside.

These conditions drive millions to migrate to the cities, whose stretched services have to cope with an influx equivalent to the population of Venezuela every year. The answer to the problems of the world's overcrowded cities, outlined in Part II, must begin in its resource-starved villages.

Poverty and dependence can be deeply humiliating. A re-searcher in a village in West Bengal found that self-respect was a high priority among those he interviewed. Some even told him that respect was more important to them than food: "without respect food won't go into the stomach."[8] If, in the words of Alan Durning, development is "the process whereby individuals and societies build the capacity to meet their own needs and improve the quality of their own lives," such human considerations are of vital importance.[9]

The next two chapters describe two holistic approaches to development in villages of the South. The first looks at the ups and downs of a Jamaican village that has maintained its self-help traditions for over half a century. The second examines the work of the Sarvodaya Shramadana Movement in thousands of villages in Sri Lanka.

Notes

1. UNDP, *Human Development Report, 1994* (New York/Oxford: Oxford University Press, 1994).
2. UNDP, *Human Development Report, 1994.*
3. Alan B. Durning, "Ending Poverty," in *State of the World 1990: Worldwatch Institute Report* (New York: W. W. Norton, 1990).
4. Robert Chambers, *Rural Development: Putting the Last First* (London: Longman Scientific and Technical, 1983); "Poverty and Livelihoods: Whose Reality Counts?" (overview paper for the UNDP Stockholm Roundtable on Global Change, July 1994).
5. Durning, "Ending Poverty."
6. UNDP, *Human Development Report, 1993* (New York/Oxford: Oxford University Press, 1993).
7. UNDP, *Human Development Report, 1994.*
8. Tony Beck, "Survival Strategies and Power Among the Poor in a West Bengal Village," *Institute of Development Studies Bulletin* 20, no. 2 (*1989*), quoted by Robert Chambers in *Poverty and Livelihoods.*
9. Alan B. Durning, "Mobilizing at the Grassroots," in *State of the World 1989: Worldwatch Institute Report* (New York: W. W. Norton, 1989), 169.

CHAPTER 2

Jamaica: The Struggle to Sustain a Miracle

The village of Walkerswood, Jamaica, has become used to being described as a miracle. It was here, in the 1940s, that Jamaica's first Pioneer Club and first cooperative farm were born, spearheading a self-help movement that embraced 236 villages by 1948.[1]

This spirit has informed all further progress, peaking in the 1970s and early 1980s, when the villagers built a community center, post office, recreational facilities, and market complex; obtained running water; and set up a number of economic enterprises. The national newspaper, the *Gleaner*, applauded each new development with an enthusiastic headline: "Walkerswood on the Move," "Walkerswood Again," "The Miracle of Walkerswood."

The village's reputation is well known all over the island— and beyond. When Chinese Vice-Premier Keng Piao visited Jamaica in 1978, he was shown Walkerswood as an example of the country's efforts at self-reliance,[2] and so was the governor-general of Canada. "Whenever you talk about community development, you talk about Walkerswood," Ed Bartlett, the government minister responsible for social development, told a British magazine in 1988.[3]

In the last thirty-five years, the population of Jamaica's cities has grown from a third to over half of the national total. By 1980, two-thirds of these city dwellers were crowded into Kingston, a city of growing shantytowns and high crime rates.[4] As in most developing countries, there is a direct link between lack of jobs

A. Edwards

Walkerswood schoolchildren outside the post office the community built for themselves

and facilities in the villages and overcrowding in the cities. The aim of Walkerswood's leaders has been to tackle the problem at the source by creating a contented, progressive, and employed rural community.

There is still a long way to go, particularly in the areas of housing and employment, and many of Walkerswood's young people leave for Kingston along the potholed main road that runs through the village. Over the years, the community has been swept to and fro in the tides of national politics and by internal conflicts and crises. When I visited the village in March 1994, community spirit was generally perceived to be at a low ebb.[5] Some of the projects set up with high hopes in preceding decades had foundered, and the community organization had been going through a period of conflict and soul-searching.

If Walkerswood has achieved miracles, its drama is about the struggle to sustain them. The players include the villagers themselves, the white family that used to own the land, foreign aid agencies, and the vicissitudes of the Jamaican economy and political fashion. One constant is the faith that underlies the motivation of most of the local people involved. "It's not easy to lead if you don't know the Lord," says one veteran. "You have to be strong to carry on."

Wind up the tortuous bends of Fern Gully from the north-coast resort of Ocho Rios and there, in the rolling hills and pastureland 1,400 feet above sea level, sits Walkerswood. The houses straggle along the narrow main road that cuts across the island to Kingston. Most of the 2,000 to 3,000 inhabitants depend on farming and jobs in the tourist industry.

In a country where 80 percent profess a Christian faith, religious conviction is a major resource. The Baptists have been in Walkerswood longest, and in October 1993, they triumphantly opened a large new church, built with their own hands. Other denominations include the Methodists, Pentecostalists, Seventh Day Adventists, and the Church of God. "This is a God-fearing place and a self-helpful place," maintains local farmer and community activist Osbourne "Apple" Francis.

Self-help goes back a long way here. The older men can remember carrying stones to school every morning as material for a new combined Methodist chapel and school, started in 1932. But the real impetus for community action came later in the decade from an unexpected source—the rebellious daughter of the landowning family who lived at Bromley, the eighteenth-century "Great House" perched on the hillside across the valley from the village.

Earlier in the century, Bromley belonged to Sir John Pringle, a Scottish doctor who had come to the British colony of Jamaica as a young man in the 1850s and ended up being one of the island's wealthiest landowners. On his death, Bromley and two other large properties passed to his daughter, Minnie. After her husband, Jim Simson, died during World War I, Minnie set up home there with her small daughter, Fiona.

Fiona grew up to manage the cattle farm and properties. She was a keen horsewoman who enjoyed the privileges wealth brought her. In 1936, alarmed by the inappropriate suitors who flocked around Fiona, Minnie took her to stay with aunts in Scotland.

While there, Fiona went to a gathering organized by the Oxford Group, the forerunner of Moral Re-Armament (MRA), which was drawing thousands to its meetings at the time. She was deeply affected by the Oxford Group's stress on seeking God's will in daily life and accepting absolute moral standards as criteria for behavior, and by the way this was linked to social and national issues. Minnie couldn't fail to be impressed by the dramatic change in her daughter's values, and any fears that she might be getting carried away by youthful religious enthusiasm were assuaged when the aunts also became involved.

When the Simsons returned home, keen to apply their newfound ideals to their life at Bromley, they made contact with other Oxford Group supporters in Jamaica. Among them were Thom and Rita Girvan, who became close friends of the Simsons. Thom Girvan was to become one of the island's most respected community workers.

The late 1930s was a period of social unrest and political awakening in Jamaica, with the formation of trade unions and political parties. In 1937, with money from the banana multinationals, Norman Manley set up an organization to promote self-help in the countryside, Jamaica Welfare. Thom Girvan joined its staff in 1939 with a brief to develop cooperatives.[6] Meanwhile, Manley had founded the People's National Party (PNP) in 1938, on the left of the political spectrum in today's polarized two-party system. (The other side, the Jamaica Labour Party [JLP], was founded in 1943.)

In 1938, land riots swept the island, and a deputation from the village turned up at Bromley, asking for land. Minnie Simson turned to the Girvans for advice. Over Sunday prayers at Bromley, Girvan met two members of the community, Peter Hinds and Alton Henry, and discussed local needs. On April 19, 1940, they founded the island's first Pioneer Club.[7]

The club met weekly for years, opening and closing with a prayer and a song or hymn, and undertaking a range of community projects, including a collective vegetable plot. Later the plot caught the eye of a government official, who arranged for its cultivators to be given land some miles away, at Lucky Hill.

The cooperative farm they established was the first of its kind in Jamaica and is still running today.[8]

"Everyone in touch with Bromley and Mrs. Minnie was fully aware of the standards of the Oxford Group," says Rita Girvan. "The men decided only married people would be allowed to own and occupy houses on the farm." The rule was significant in a country where slaves had once been prohibited from marrying and where 70 percent of babies are still born out of wedlock. Even today, one of Walkerswood's aims is to create an environment where people feel secure enough to settle down. "It's indisputable that leadership in the village has come from people who are part of a stable family structure," says Minnie's grandson, Roddy Edwards.

The ethos of Jamaica Welfare and the Pioneer Clubs was Christian and service oriented. "A distinctive feature of the [Walkerswood] club was the bond that tied its members together with a very strong sense of duty, not only to the club, but to the development of the country," writes Maxine Henry-Wilson in a recent case study of Walkerswood.[9] Jamaica Welfare adopted a theme song written by Mary MacNicol, one of the Scottish aunts, during a visit to Bromley. Both its stirring tone and its message, linking the personal and the national, were typical of the Oxford Group:

> We work so Jamaica shall truly be great
> An island where God has command.
> An end shall be put to division and hate,
> New unity sweep thro' the land.
> No more shall a sectoral selfishness reign,
> No more shall the workless seek labor in vain,
> We'll work as a team with one goal—
> Jamaica with God in control.

In 1948, Jamaica Welfare became the Jamaica Social Welfare Commission, funded by the government. By then it embraced 1,180 groups that were active in 236 villages. Thom Girvan's son, economist Norman Girvan, writes, "Tangible accomplishments aside, perhaps the most important aspect of the impact of Welfare was the sense of empowerment, of hope and of participation in nation-building that it engendered among the previously neglected rural population."[10] The broader vision of creating a model for the nation, as well as meeting local needs, continued to be a driving force in Walkerswood's efforts over the decades.

The Pioneer Club gave birth to a partnership between the family at Bromley and the community that observers maintain is unique. Rita Girvan says that Minnie Simson was the first of Jamaica's rich white plantocracy to open her doors to black people on the basis of friendship and equality. But it went beyond socializing. In most projects in Walkerswood, there has been a Bromley input in terms of land, finance, or support. The involvement has been sustained through three generations: Minnie Simson, who died in 1980; Fiona and her husband, John Edwards; and their sons Jonathan and Roddy.

Facing Bromley across the valley is a row of neat white cottages, built by the estate's workers on land given to them by Minnie Simson. Next door to each other live brothers Victor and David Henry, both committed Methodists. They were young men when their namesake, Alton Henry, helped found the Pioneer Club and moved to Lucky Hill. Victor, who has headed every community organization since, didn't get involved. "I saw the Pioneer Club as hard labor and monkey allowance [bad pay]," he says.

His chance came in the 1950s and 1960s, as head of the Parent-Teacher Association (PTA), which replaced the Pioneer Club as the impetus for community action. By then, the use of the Methodist church as a school was causing problems. At the PTA's request, Minnie Simson, who had given land for a school garden, went to the relevant government minister in Kingston and insisted that a school be built on this land. According to Rita Girvan, he agreed without a murmur. "She was very quiet, but very forceful."

The all-age school opened in 1967. Built for 180 children aged six to fifteen, it now houses 328. Meanwhile, the PTA had become convinced of the need for a community hall. It rallied the villagers, who pooled their resources and built it themselves, setting a pattern for future communal projects. Within a couple of years, the hall was being used as a "basic" school for children under six.

Walkerswood's greatest period of expansion and optimism began in the early 1970s, when Fiona's sons, Jonathan and Roddy, returned to Jamaica from education and work overseas, determined to put something back into the community. The social and political climate was in their favor. Independence had come to the island in 1962. In 1972, Michael Manley, son of Norman, came to power as the head of a PNP government. He shared the social welfare and development ideology of his father, but his orientation was further to the left. It was to be a decade of turmoil for Jamaica, with aid donors and prosperous Jamaicans taking flight from Manley's left-wing leanings. But it provided a fair wind for a community with a desire to take its destiny into its own hands.

A study of Walkerswood written by Linton Gordon in 1975 paints a grim picture of a community crippled by a lack of land and jobs.[11] The population depended on subsistence farming, much of it accomplished by squatting on land owned by the bauxite company, Reynolds Jamaica Mines (RJM). Although the company owned most of the land, it employed only nineteen villagers and eventually pulled out in 1984. "The high propensity to leave Walkerswood for other towns in search of jobs is a result of the lack of job opportunities outside of subsistence farming which is in a permanent state of stagnation," commented Gordon. Only six of the village's 281 homes had water tanks, and only twenty-four had water closets. Those without water had to buy it from the six tank owners, collect it from the unhygienic public tank, or help themselves—at some risk—from ponds on RJM land. The nearest doctor and clinic were four miles away in Moneague, and the community had no sporting facilities.

Reinforced by the Edwards brothers, the PTA set about addressing these concerns. Jonathan, a natural leader, worked

J. Hairs

From left: Lurene Ellis, Roddy Edwards, and Woody Mitchell in Walkerswood's cafe

with the Henrys, Osbourne Francis, and others on the communal concerns. Roddy took on the economic portfolio, exploring ways of creating jobs locally.

With government encouragement, Walkerswood set up a community council, with Jonathan as chairman and Victor Henry as a vice-chairman. In December 1976, after a long campaign by their local government representative, Cyril Miller, running water was piped to the community for the first time from a well dug by the National Water Authority on land donated by Minnie Simson. The same year, work began on a multipurpose community center on land donated by RJM. "We called a meeting at the school," remembers David Henry. "Some said they would give twenty blocks, others a few dollars." Finance also came from the government, but the community did the work itself, fortified by huge pots of soup made from anything people cared to throw in.

For Woodrow (Woody) Mitchell, secretary of the new council, these were stirring days. He had been paralyzed in a car accident in 1972, had seen "all [his] dreams go out of the window," but had fought through to the belief that he could still make a contribution, even from a wheelchair. "When they started building the community center I got really excited," he says. "The community was so motivated." The project came in under budget, and on April 26, 1979, a huge crowd turned out in the pouring rain to see Michael Manley open the center with its auditorium, clinic, craft workshops, and playing fields. The clinic was staffed by a doctor from RJM, and nurses provided prenatal and infant care.

In 1979, Jonathan Edwards left to settle in the United States, but Walkerswood seemed unstoppable. In 1983, its Women's Center opened with a thrift shop, space for training courses and a day-care center, and, most useful of all, a kerosene tank. This meant that people no longer had to travel four miles to buy fuel, a journey exacerbated by the sparseness of public buses. That same year, the village post office came under threat of closure, and the community decided to build its own. "It began as a dream," gushed the *Sunday Gleaner* in October 1984. "Today, one year later, it is a beautiful reality . . . a building put up by themselves, block by block, with hardly a cent paid out for labor."[12]

Meanwhile, under the auspices of the employment committee of the community council, a number of economic enterprises had opened. "The fundamental belief was that no sustainable community development could take place unless an adequate number of people had steady jobs over which they had some control," says Roddy Edwards. With the help of an American Peace Corps volunteer, a group of women revived a wool spinners' cooperative, first begun in the 1930s, and a British wood turner arrived to train local men in his craft. Roddy Edwards and Calvin Hunter, a youth leader, started a cottage industry producing jerk pork, a Jamaican specialty, with the help of a dedicated government food technologist. Later they moved to Bromley and bought out a confectionary business that had been started by Roddy's father. They experimented with a number of products and, by the mid-1980s, were exporting jerk seasoning to Britain. To capture passing customers for these businesses and for local farmers, the community raised the money from aid donors to build a market complex at the center of the village.

In 1980, Manley's socialist government was replaced by the more private enterprise–oriented JLP government of Edward Seaga. Community councils, tainted by their PNP genesis, were seen as "communist" organizations. To escape these associations, the community council reconstituted itself in 1984 as the Walkerswood Community Development Foundation, but conflict continued in the community. This was partially resolved at a "peace conference," at which one of the youth leaders apologized to the new JLP member of parliment because he had treated her badly.

By the mid-1980s, Walkerswood certainly looked like a success story. Aid agencies, including Oxfam and the Canadian International Development Agency (CIDA), were eager to assist it, and the community had to turn down offers. The community had built up a good track record of honesty and giving value for money, says Woody Mitchell. Its relative political neutrality helped too.

"It's difficult to find places to support because so many are politicized," the Caribbean representative of the Inter-American Foundation, Julie Sutphen, explained at the time. "At Walkerswood they've gone beyond rhetoric and done it themselves. With our budget we can't solve problems with money. We have to find organizations like Walkerswood that provide an example for others."[13]

"The Walkerswood story has all the elements of a development journalist's perfect motivational soap opera," commented Selena Tapper, Caribbean representative of Canadian Universities Service Overseas (CUSO), in 1988. "There is the white family in the Great House, passing down through the dynasty, not a lust for power, but a sense of fellowship, benevolence, belonging; a young, handsome black hero, tragically crippled in an accident but rising above it; a close-knit circle of wise elders; caring fathers; women taking leadership roles." It seemed malicious, she continued, "to look for serpents in the apple groves." But in the face of Jamaica's lack of housing, employment, transport, and housing, she saw problems ahead. "The way forward depends on finding a way to mobilize the next generation."

Walkerswood's achievements are real. In a 1989 study for Jamaica's Institute of Social and Economic Research, Ian Boxill wrote that he had "found no community organization which compares with the independent strides made by Walkerswood within the last two decades."[14] Few similar communities in Jamaica have addressed so many of their universal needs—from running water to burial grounds. By national standards, crime is low.

Up on the hill at Bromley, Cottage Industries is thriving under the strong management of Woody Mitchell. It now exports preserves, spices, and sauces to North America and Europe and had a turnover in 1993 of J$17.5 million (US$580,000). It employs thirty-five permanent and a varying number of temporary staff, all but two of them from the village, and buys raw materials from local farmers. It has twenty-one shareholders, all past or present employees, and is the only community-based rural agro-industry of its size on the island. There are plans to build a new factory.

In spite of this, when I visited Walkerswood in 1994, the prevailing mood was one of disappointment that the dreams of the glory days had not been realized. The community center, once the pride of the village, is underutilized and run-down after the ravages of Hurricane Gilbert in 1988. The market complex is also underused: local farmers felt safer sticking with assured markets eight miles away in Ocho Rios, in spite of the transport costs. The restaurant and supermarket are struggling. The wool spinners have given up amid accusations of misappropriated funds. But two of the wood turners and a wickerworker are still at work; a flourishing crafts business employs three people; and Victor Henry's Rastafarian son, Ras Fikre, runs a fruit stall.

The Walkerswood Community Development Foundation has had its difficulties too. Few turn out for meetings except at moments of crisis, and its relations with the community have been bedeviled by mistrust. In 1986, disagreements over who should go on an exchange with a youth club in Brixton, London, led to a rift between the youth and the leadership of the community. Dark (and unfounded) rumors began to circulate that the foundation leadership was lining its own pockets, and "White boy go home" appeared on the restaurant door in a specific attack on Roddy Edwards. Wrangles over rents for the use of community property drove a newly hired manager to resign in frustration after only eight months on the job. A packed meeting howled down proposals to create jobs by building a hotel on community land, on the grounds that its presence would inhibit people's "freeness." The old guard stepped down and the youth voted in a young president, who quickly left when he found that the job was beyond him.

Mitchell is philosophical about the changeover. "You have to expect cycles: peaks and valleys," he says. He welcomes the breather after nearly twenty years of community involvement. "I'll get back in there when I've satisfied some of the selfish objectives I've set myself." Edwards agrees: "It was time for others who felt we'd done badly to have a chance to get on with it. Throughout Jamaican history people have hung on too long. And there's a genuine sense of exhaustion in any group that has been in power for a number of years." And he believes that the voters of Walkerswood have been shrewd. "The youth wanted a young president, but when it came to holding the purse strings, the community voted in a tried and tested treasurer who had a managerial post at Cottage Industries."

Many of the older generation blame the community's troubles on the decadence of today's youth. "We used to be round-the-clock volunteers," says Osbourne Francis. "The younger people of today want money up front." Young people today resent being taught, maintains Ras Fikre, who coaches the community's football team.

Part of the problem is that times have changed. Inflation runs at 22.1 percent (1993 figures), and the Jamaican dollar has fallen in value—from 5 to the U.S. dollar in 1991 to 30 in 1993. People are finding it hard to make ends meet. And the mood in the country, as in the world, has swung away from cooperation toward individualism.

Mitchell reckons that the disaffection began when the foundation moved from communal work on facilities that would benefit everybody to paid work on structures, such as the market complex, that would benefit a few. "It was a deliberate policy at the time because we were trying to provide employment opportunities," he says. "But there was a lot of money around, and it had a draining effect. There was jealousy and suspicion."

Ian Boxill came to similar conclusions. The economic enterprises made people think that the foundation's aim was to make money, he wrote. "It is probably advisable in embarking on large-scale economic projects to ensure that a balance is struck with the human aspects of community development (e.g. sport)." In general, he continued, there is a need for research on how community organizations can adapt to changes in attitudes and demands in the communities they serve.[15]

"Given that the political direction in the country was against us, we should have spent more time on training people," says Edwards. "We were too focused on the economic thing. Like many other people in the early 1980s, we had become convinced of the need for individual initiative to create resources rather than the more centrally planned communal approach. Perhaps we went rather overboard on this." One of the main problems with the wool spinners and wood turners seems to have been a lack of strong management and marketing.

Much of the recent ill feeling has focused on the role of Bromley, personified by Edwards, in the foundation and in Cottage Industries. In 1991, Maxine Henry-Wilson, then a lecturer at the University of the West Indies and later a minister of state in the prime minister's office, produced a case study on the community. She found some young people attacking Cottage Industries as "a new form of 'colonialism and slavery,'" with Edwards as master. Younger employees told her that their peers harassed them for working there.[16]

Woody Mitchell is impatient with such arguments, listing the ways that Bromley has helped the community. "If Great Houses in other communities had played such a positive role, we'd have quite a few more Walkerswoods." Boxill too cites access to assistance from Bromley as one of the reasons for Walkerswood's relative success. But Selena Tapper, writing in 1988, believed that the time had come for initiative to switch from the Great House to the community. The Edwards family agrees.

For Roddy Edwards, one of the main lessons of twenty years in Walkerswood has been to accept the validity of other people's aims. "People's aspirations are infinite in their variety." He was surprised, for instance, when some Cottage Industries workers turned down the offer of share ownership. "Their objective was to earn their wages without the risk or worry of responsibility: they have risks and worries in other areas of life. This is where the more force-fed type of legalistic egalitarianism I used to be enamored of didn't mesh with life itself. I had to learn through practice that activism by a minority, however well-intentioned, was inadequate. Villages are made up of diverse groups, with all sorts of different and constantly shifting agendas. Leadership at every level needs to be encouraged."

When Edwards returned to Jamaica in the 1970s, he brought with him two fundamental tenets learned in six years' voluntary work in Ethiopia, India, and the West: the search "to discern the will of God in all I am involved in" and the belief that "I have a better chance of being an agent of change if I am prepared to start with myself." He tempers the first with the recognition that discernment involves listening to other people: no one person ever has access to the whole truth. But he believes that any group working together needs some form of higher authority. "It can be profit (though that isn't much good in community work), brute force, liberal values, a charismatic leader, or it can be God."

Many of the key players in Walkerswood share this approach, though they might express it differently. David Henry looks back on his days as a young cattleman when the community used to gather for prayers. "We have contention and we quarrel. We have some very botheration workers." Differences were often settled, he says, after quiet reflection.

"What advice would I give to another community?" muses Lurene Ellis, an executive member of the foundation, a staunch Baptist, and a community stalwart. "It's good to have some community group and it is wise to let people be free to speak. The leaders have to be strong and God-fearing to take criticism. In most of our meetings, people get hot and throw words. It's wise not to adjourn until you can be friends. And if people leave because they feel hurt, you have to keep on at them until they come back."

Similar philosophies prevail at Cottage Industries. "Every month we have a workers' meeting," says production coordinator Denyse Perkins. "Anyone can come up with an idea—it could be the person who's sweeping the floor, it could be Roddy or Woody. People aren't afraid to make suggestions. We listen to them." That morning, a deadlock had yielded when she apologized to one of the workers for the tone in which she had asked him to do a job.

The resentment in the community seems to have bottomed out. A few activities are springing up through the foundation. Some people are coming back to the idea of the hotel. A labor day at the center drew a good response, and there were plans to have a summer program for the children for the second year running. A housing scheme projected for the outskirts of the village should bring new blood and new money into the community, although the prices mean that it will do nothing to meet Walkerswood's housing needs. "I await a renewal of spirit both in me and in the community—and I think it's going to happen," says Mitchell.

Walkerswood's experience illustrates the issues facing any community that tries to sustain a spirit of self-help over half a century. It is obvious that there are going to be highs and lows: the excitement, energy, and solidarity generated at different times by the building of the basic school, community center, and post office were bound to ease off once the projects were completed. As times change and young people grow up, taking their parents' achievements for granted, intergenerational tensions are inevitable.

This is where the spiritual genesis of the Walkerswood experiment comes in. Those involved—both at Bromley and in the community—have had something deeper to sustain them than material success—a constancy of purpose that has helped them through national upheavals and changes of fashion. Two of the legacies of the Oxford Group have been particularly significant: a vision of creating a model for the nation, and a means of conflict resolution through accepting that change begins in oneself. The latter has given Walkerswood a flexibility that is not always conspicuous in belief-driven initiatives. The community has also managed to be nonpartisan in its politics, a quality that appeals to grant donors.

No community is an island. Walkerswood achieved "miracles" in the 1940s and 1970s when national trends supported and encouraged community development. But it has also managed to make progress when the wind has not been blowing its way. Thanks to a remarkable partnership between classes and colors and to a continuity of leadership, principles, and visions, a small village in Jamaica has created facilities and job opportunities enjoyed by few other rural communities on the island. And that, whatever the current problems, is a miracle in itself.

Notes

1. D. T. M. Girvan, *Working Together for Development*, edited by Norman Girvan (Kingston: Institute of Jamaica Publications, 1993).
2. *Daily Gleaner*, July 22, 1978.
3. Michael Henderson, "It Takes Two Hands to Clap," *For a Change*, April 1988.
4. UNDP, *Human Development Report, 1993* (New York/Oxford: Oxford University Press, 1993).
5. During ten days in Jamaica in March 1994, I interviewed a wide range of people in Walkerswood and Kingston, including Fiona, Roddy, and Ann Edwards; Lurene Ellis; Ras Fikre; Osbourne Francis; Rita Girvan; Sheila Graham; Lileth Guy; David Henry; Martin Henry; Victor and Alvis Henry; Joyce Hinds; Carol Lindo; Woody Mitchell; Denyse Perkins; Stanley Simpson; Selena Tapper; and Trevor Williams. I am grateful to Michael

Henderson for making available the notes from his interviews in 1987–88. Unreferenced quotes are taken from my own, or Henderson's, interviews.

6. Girvan, *Working Together*.
7. Girvan, *Working Together*.
8. *The Welfare Reporter*, April 1948, quoted in Girvan.
9. Maxine Henry-Wilson, "Case Study: Walkerswood," May 1991.
10. Girvan, *Working Together*, 220.
11. Linton Gordon, "Study of Walkerswood" (bachelor's dissertation, University of the West Indies, 1975).
12. *Sunday Gleaner*, October 7, 1984.
13. Julie Sutphen, interview with Michael Henderson, January 20, 1988.
14. Ian Boxill, "Case Studies of Walkerswood Community Development Foundation and August Town Community Council" (Jamaican Institute of Social and Economic Research project on grassroots democracy, 1989).
15. Boxill, "Case Studies."
16. Henry-Wilson, "Case Study."

CHAPTER 3

Self-Reliance
in Sri Lanka's Villages

The island of Sri Lanka is home to one of the world's best-known spiritual approaches to community development, the Sarvodaya Shramadana Movement.[1] Over the last forty years, it has taken its message of twofold liberation—change in the inner person and in the outer structures of society—to up to 7,000 of the country's 23,000 villages.[2] Its achievements demonstrate the power of spiritual values as a resource in development.

Sarvodaya started out in the mid-1950s as an informal volunteer group relying on indigenous resources. By 1992, it had grown to an estimated 7,000 full-time staff and volunteers,[3] and its work was largely financed by overseas aid. This expansion imposed constraints on the movement that have deflected it from some of its early aims and illustrate some of the pitfalls that accompany growth and success.[4]

Nearly four-fifths of Sri Lanka's 17.7 million people are villagers. The gulf between town and country is narrower than in many countries of the South, but over a third of Sri Lanka's villagers still have no safe water supply, and over two-fifths have no sanitation (all city dwellers have access to clean water and nearly three-quarters to sanitation). Literacy rates are high, with nine-tenths of the country's population able to read and write short statements.[5] But each year, over half the country's income goes into the pockets of just a tenth of its population.[6]

Sri Lanka regained independence in 1948, after 450 years of Portuguese, Dutch, and British rule. In recent decades, the country has been torn by strife between its Sinhalese (mostly Buddhist) majority and its Tamil (mostly Hindu) minority. In 1989, it suffered more political murders per capita than any other country in the world.[7] The country is ruled by a city-based, English-speaking elite and is heavily dependent on exporting tea, rubber, and coconut grown on plantations.

Sarvodaya was created in a remote village in 1958, at a two-week work camp for high school students from the capital, Colombo. It was organized by a group of teachers who thought that the postcolonial education system was too classroom- and city-based, with little relevance to the real challenges facing the country. Their aim, wrote one of the teachers, was to help their pupils "understand and experience the true state of affairs that prevailed in the rural and poor urban areas . . . [and] to develop a love for their people and utilize the education they received to find ways of building a more just and happier life for them."[8] The idea caught on, and soon hundreds of students were taking part in similar *shramadana* (labor-giving) camps in the rural areas.

As the Shramadana Movement grew, its emphasis changed from widening the horizons of students to helping villagers develop themselves. Its prime mover, A. T. Ariyaratne, went to India to work with the Gandhian rural development pioneer Vinobha Bhave and returned with the concept of *sarvodaya* (a word coined by Gandhi and originally meaning the "welfare of all," but interpreted by Ariyaratne as the "awakening of all"). In 1961, Ariyaratne launched the Sarvodaya Shramadana Movement. His wife, Neetha, resigned her job as a teacher and became its first full-time worker.

Sarvodaya's aim, according to its organizers, has been to create a no-poverty, no-affluence society based on a spiritual reawakening in individuals. Drawing on Buddhist and Gandhian teaching, its philosophy sees material development as a means, not an end: its emphasis is on development of the whole person. "Sarvodaya stresses the development of social, psychological, religious as well as economic factors," writes Hans Wismeijer. "According to the Sarvodaya ideology, any development

Sarvodaya

A. T. Ariyaratne, founder of Sri Lanka's Sarvodaya Shramadana Movement

effort which concentrates on only one of these factors while neglecting the others is doomed to failure."[9]

"Unless social change is brought about by people who are changed and uplifted in their hearts, they will merely be exchanging one set of problems for another, exchanging injustice for injustice, terror for terror and hatred for hatred," maintains

Sarvodaya worker Jehan Perera.[10] The idea is that an awakening of all, at all levels of society, will lead to a just and nonviolent country, where each community has maximum control over its own destiny.

In a paper presented at a conference on poverty alleviation in 1991, Sarvodaya rejected the Western model of development as unbalanced, exploitative of natural resources, profit oriented, and greed driven. "This has brought affluence to a small section of the world's population . . . and poverty and powerlessness to the vast majority." By contrast, Sarvodaya has aimed "to create a society that is neither rich nor poor, and where the latest advances in science in concert with traditional wisdom are utilized so that every individual, family and community is awakened to a more contented, peaceful and just life."[11]

When the village of Rilhena got in touch with Sarvodaya in 1983, its people had been waiting for three years for the government to keep a promise to supply them with clean water. "We realized that our power was not in Colombo; it had to be with us," explained Kanthi, one of the young mothers who invited Sarvodaya's representative to the village.

As in most Sarvodaya villages, change in Rilhena began with a series of community meetings, where the villagers agreed to organize a *shramadana* camp to sink tube wells supplied by a foreign donor. The two-day camp also gave the villagers a chance to learn how to maintain the wells. Working together strengthened their esprit de corps and encouraged them to go on to the next step in Sarvodaya's program—the establishment of mothers', youth, children's, farmers', and elders' groups that cut across caste, class, and political party. These groups went on to found their own independent Sarvodaya Society, with the legal power to own land, obtain loans, and set up economic enterprises.

Rilhena's mothers' group persuaded the villagers to hold a second *shramadana* camp to build a preschool. The children got a daily meal, with the help of a foreign-sponsored food aid scheme. Their teacher was a villager who was trained at the Sarvodaya district center and worked for no pay. Nationwide,

Sarvodaya

A shramadana camp: "we build the road, and the road builds us"

Sarvodaya's preschool program has helped over 300,000 small children.[12] The village also set up a cashew nut processing business. "If we are given a chance we can develop ourselves," Kanthi told a Sarvodaya researcher proudly.

The villagers of Thengedagedera might echo her words. In the mid-1970s, the bund (embankment) around the small reservoir that feeds its paddy fields collapsed. The community could not raise the 15,000 rupees (US$450) to repair it, and for the next fifteen years they had no water in the dry season and no second harvest.

In 1989, with Sarvodaya help, the villagers organized a *shramadana* camp to repair the bund. Three hundred people from Thengedagedera and thereabouts took part. The job was done in a day: the visitors brought their own tools, the villagers fed them, there was no need to hire a bulldozer, and no money changed hands. "In sharing their labor, the villagers found their relationships to one another were being transformed," comments Jehan Perera. "Class, caste, and other divisions yielded to the sense of participation in a shared endeavor. As the Sarvodaya saying goes, 'We build the road, the road builds us.'"

Shramadana camps are the heart of the Sarvodaya process—the moment when a village comes together and discovers its own strength. Between 1972 and 1982, Sarvodaya helped organize some 13,700 camps;[13] between 1986 and 1990, 20,000 camps took place, involving 1.4 million people.[14] In 1982, Sarvodaya estimated that in one year its camps had laid three times more road than the government had, at one-eighteenth of the cost.[15]

The method has been so successful that it has been taken up by government agencies as well. But according to Joanna Macy in her study of Sarvodaya,[16] these copy camps tended to be less effective than the originals. The unique thing about Sarvodaya's camps, she writes, was that they were a local initiative, drawing on local labor, and that they included everyone in the community, regardless of age or sex. Even the smallest gift in kind was valued. Asked about one giver, a camp organizer replied, "Of course her family is poor and of course we do not really need her little bit of rice or her betel leaf. But in giving it, she gets a new idea about herself."[17]

Sarvodaya's efforts have a strong religious component, drawing on local traditions. In the 1970s and early 1980s in particular, many Buddhist monks were involved. Their presence, and the religious context of Sarvodaya proceedings, made it easier for village women to take part.

During a classic *shramadana*, as described by Macy, the participants stop work three times a day for a "family meeting" with meditation, chants, and prayers. At these occasions, even women and young people feel free to speak out. Each contribution is greeted with identical applause to confer equal dignity on each person. Through working together and eating together, the villagers discover their united potential.

The *shramadana* camp, she writes, is "an island in time when villagers can see themselves and each other in a new light." She quotes a Sarvodaya district organizer: "The road we build may wash away, but the attitudes we build do not." Whereas many for-the-people projects suffer neglect, by-the-people projects confer a sense of ownership and responsibility. "When the government builds a school or community center, people have gone in the night to steal the hinges off the doors," says a school principal. "When people build by *shramadana*, nothing is touched— they even go to repair it, as if it were their own home."[18]

Sarvodaya backs up village initiatives with its expertise in organizing camps and determining the feasibility of proposed projects. Over the years, it has provided training for community leaders and access to loans, savings, and legal aid; developed a range of appropriate technologies, from windmills to mortar made out of banana tree sap; and run an array of income-generating programs. Its Children's Home Gardening, Children's Fairs, and Savings Program encouraged three- to fifteen-year-olds to grow vegetables and fruit, sell them at specially organized fairs, and save the proceeds through the local Sarvodaya office. By 1991, when a change in banking laws forced the scheme to close down, the program had 190,000 savers.

The enthusiasm of Sarvodaya's workers has been central to its success. In the early days, people worked without pay; later, they received a basic living allowance way below the market wage rate. In these circumstances, the incentive for enlisting with Sarvodaya was conviction rather than economic ambition.

Jehan Perera, a Harvard graduate and former Davis Cup tennis player, is an example. In 1990, after working with Sarvodaya for three years, he had the chance to take a U.N. job that was tailor-made to his qualifications at six times the $200-a-month salary he was receiving. "The great advantage of material things is that they are visible," he says. "My friends had these visible signs of success. I did not. But in the end, the more idealistic part of me triumphed." He stayed on with Sarvodaya.[19]

The spirit of Sarvodaya still has the power to inspire sacrifice and commitment, but in recent years, this spirit has been tested. One cause of the movement's malaise has been its phenomenal growth. For the first fifteen years of its existence, Sarvodaya was locally funded, mostly by donations from villagers. It responded to requests from villages with the skills and time of its volunteers and acted as a link between people who needed help and those who could provide it. Ariyaratne supported the first full-time workers out of his teacher's salary until he resigned in 1972.

By then, Sarvodaya was active in 300 villages. To respond to all the requests for help it had begun to run training programs and had set up an administrative headquarters at Moratuwa, outside Colombo. In the early 1970s, the first foreign donors entered the picture. Their contributions made it possible for Sarvodaya to extend its activities to 2,000 villages by 1977 and to employ 2,000 full-time workers.[20]

In 1983, as the country slid toward civil war, Sarvodaya continued to work with both Tamil and Sinhalese communities, in areas where government structures were collapsing. This made it an attractive channel for foreign agencies that were keen to provide relief to those caught in the cross fire. Sarvodaya suddenly found itself handling much larger sums of money: between 1983 and 1987, the funds passing through its hands quadrupled.[21] Although it still saw its major role as acting as a catalyst for change, it found itself becoming an aid-disbursing agency as well.

By 1985, over 80 percent of Sarvodaya's budget came from overseas.[22] A movement that had preached self-reliance now found itself in the embarrassing position of depending on foreign aid. Ariyaratne justified this by emphasizing the vast non-monetary resources that Sri Lankans contributed to Sarvodaya in terms of labor and gifts in kind and by pointing to the impossibility of complete self-reliance in a radically unequal world. Sarvodaya's supporters pointed out that the movement benefited Sri Lanka's economy by bringing in foreign resources to be spent on local goods and services.

The volume of funds also had an impact on Sarvodaya's character, structure, and way of doing things. "The donors were all keen to help Sarvodaya, but in so doing they transformed what had been a people organization into a more administrative organization," says Alan Todd, who worked with Sarvodaya in the early 1990s.[23] "Though the spiritual message was still there, people began to come to it for the money, not the message." Within Sarvodaya itself, former volunteers became dependent on the financial support that the movement could now provide.

Because its message was holistic, Sarvodaya had always seen itself as a model of the sort of Sri Lanka it wanted to create—decentralized, village led, and nonmaterialistic. These ideals became harder to sustain as the movement grew and began to supply more and more services in-house. With foreign aid came the need to provide reports and assessments to reassure donors that their money was being well spent. This led to the growth of a bureaucracy and, in time, to a more centralized hierarchical form of organization, which took power away from the village-level societies that were supposed to be the movement's true leaders.

Because few of Sarvodaya's field workers had training in administration, the donors also pressed for professionals to be brought in from outside to work at headquarters. This was already causing friction in 1982 and 1984, when Wismeijer was researching his dissertation for the University of Utrecht.[24] He found ill feeling toward the new professionals, who were better paid than the original Sarvodaya workers but not always as close to the movement's values. This internal tension increased over the next ten years as more outsiders were brought in. The underpaid volunteers began to feel that their idealism was being exploited. Communication between the increasingly professionalized headquarters and the people on the ground in the villages began to break down. Morale plummeted and a low-pay, low-discipline, low-performance culture began to emerge.

The donors' justifiable need for accountability, and their narrow interpretation of what this meant, also caused problems. "They want to evaluate less than 50 percent of our activities," a senior Sarvodayan told Wismeijer in the early 1980s. "They want to know all about our economic activities, our political activities and part of our social activities. But they completely ignore the moral, cultural and spiritual elements, which are part and parcel of our approach to development. Such elements do not fit into [the] Western rational way of thinking. . . . We would not know how to evaluate our nonmaterial achievements in a way that satisfies Western scientific standards. But that does not mean that such achievements are nonexistent."[25]

Alan Todd, who was Sarvodaya's liaison with the donors in 1992–93, sees the problem as a fundamental culture clash. "The idea that everything can be measured is totally at odds with the approach of the East," he says. "It was a case of people in the West trying to impose their own values." The situation was complicated by cultural misunderstanding: when donors visited, they would interpret smiling silence as acquiescence rather than noncommittal politeness; Sarvodayans were sometimes reluctant to admit that they did not understand what the donors were asking for.

By the late 1980s, writes Simon Zadek, "the bureaucracy associated with accountability to funders had over-ridden the powerful grassroots processes that had originally informed the direction of the movement."[26] Alarmed by the inefficiency and ineffectiveness of the bureaucracy they had helped to create, the donors enlisted a succession of overseas consultants to advise on streamlining, but with little effect.

Alongside its organizational crisis, Sarvodaya was also locked in a struggle with the government of Sri Lanka, dating from the elections of 1989, when Ranasinghe Premadasa became president. A book published in 1992 chronicles a series of controversies, attacks in the government-owned press, harassments, death threats, and obstructions designed to prejudice Sarvodaya's chances before a presidential commission investigating Sri Lanka's nongovernmental organizations (NGOs).[27] The storm of accusations put off some donors, forcing Sarvodaya to close down several programs, including its legal aid program. The attacks, which were fueled partly by Ariyaratne's political ambitions and by the president's distrust of his popularity, stopped after Premadasa's assassination in May 1993, but political problems continue.

In spite of the developing crisis at headquarters, Sarvodaya's work in the countryside continued, and *shramadana* camps still took place. "The spiritual emphasis of the original Sarvodaya had been much reduced," maintains Alan Todd. "But away from the center, in the local communities, the roots were strong. That is where you found the real spirit of Sarvodaya." As I write, however, Sarvodaya is in financial crisis, with diminishing donor support, and its future hangs in the balance.

When Sarvodaya took off over thirty years ago, it broke new ground by listening to the disadvantaged and turning its back on the sort of top-down charitable giving that fosters dependency. As it expanded, however, it found itself forced into patterns of organization that mirrored the inefficient, hierarchical structures of which it had been so critical.

Some of its problems have been of its own making: like any other burgeoning movement based on personal belief, a charismatic leader, and a loose organizational structure, it has been vulnerable to charges of lack of accountability. Its consensus approach to decision making, based in part on reverence for Ariyaratne, has made it hard for constructive criticism to surface from within the movement. It was unrealistic to imagine that outsiders could be brought in at higher rates of pay without demoralizing the lower-paid volunteers and driving away those who felt that they would be better valued elsewhere. And the belief that development is about personal growth in all who are involved in the process, Sarvodaya staff included, may have led to overtolerance of mistakes and abuses. Sarvodayans speak with pride and exasperation about the time Ariyaratne promoted a staff member who had stolen from the organization to a position with greater financial responsibilities, in the hope that this would encourage him to reform.[28]

Other problems are inherent in the process of growth and in the culture clash between the West and the East. Zadek and Szabo exonerate the donors of malice but point to the risks involved in such contacts for NGOs in general: "An overdrive towards particular forms of efficiency will reduce NGOs to little more than service delivery agents, and probably not very efficient ones at that."[29] They point out the need for NGOs like Sarvodaya to evolve convincing means of self-evaluation that relate to their values and goals and go beyond purely material criteria.

Sarvodaya's early days, and its enduring aspirations, offer an ideal of holistic, bottom-up development in which, in Ariyaratne's words, "the individual's mental make-up, and the social environment in which he lives are both undergoing revolution."[30] As with all ideals, it has been hard to realize. Sarvodaya's practice probably always fell short of its philosophy. But that does not invalidate the boldness of the original experiment nor the importance of the worldview on which it was based.

Notes

1. This chapter draws on the studies of Sarvodaya cited below and on conversations and correspondence (unreferenced) with Wim Aspeslagh, Jehan Perera, Alan Todd, and Simon Zadek.
2. Simon Zadek and Sue Szabo, *Valuing Organisation: The Case of Sarvodaya* (London: New Economics Foundation, 1994).
3. Jehan Perera, Charika Marasinghe, and Leela Jayasekera, *A People's Movement Under Siege* (Colombo: Sarvodaya Publications, 1992).
4. These difficulties erupted into crisis in late 1994, and the situation is so volatile as I write that any description is in danger of losing currency before this book is published. For that reason, I have concentrated on Sarvodaya's evolution and struggles in the years up to 1993.
5. UNDP, *Human Development Report, 1994* (New York/Oxford: Oxford University Press, 1994).
6. Jehan Perera, "We Build the Road, the Road Builds Us," *For a Change*, April 1990.
7. Perera, "We Build the Road."
8. Joanna Macy, *Dharma and Development: Religion as Resource in the Sarvodaya Self-Help Movement*, rev. ed. (West Hartford, Conn.: Kumarian Press, 1985), 24.
9. Hans Wismeijer, *From Charisma to Bureaucracy? Organization and Ideology in the Sarvodaya Shramadana Movement in Sri Lanka* (Utrecht: ICAU Mededeling, 1986), 3.
10. Jehan Perera, talk to Studies in Effective Living course, Melbourne, Australia, 1990.
11. Perera, Marasinghe, and Jayasekera, *People's Movement Under Siege*, 146.
12. Perera, Marasinghe, and Jayasekera, *People's Movement Under Siege*.
13. Macy, *Dharma and Development*.
14. Perera, "We Build the Road."
15. Macy, *Dharma and Development*.
16. Macy, *Dharma and Development*.
17. Macy, *Dharma and Development*, 38.
18. Macy, *Dharma and Development*, 52, 54, 95.
19. Perera, Melbourne, 1990.

20. Wismeijer, *From Charisma to Bureaucracy?*
21. Zadek and Szabo, *Valuing Organization.*
22. Macy, *Dharma and Development.*
23. In 1986, four major donors, the Netherlands Organisation for International Cooperation (NOVIB), the Canadian International Development Agency (CIDA), the British Overseas Development Administration (ODA), and the Norwegian Government International Cooperation Agency (NORAD), formed a consortium for working with Sarvodaya.
24. Wismeijer, *From Charisma to Bureaucracy?*
25. Wismeijer, *From Charisma to Bureaucracy?*, 323.
26. Simon Zadek, "Coping with Value-Based Viruses," (New Economics Foundation paper, 1994).
27. Perera, Marasinghe, and Jayasekera, *People's Movement Under Siege.* Coauthor Charika Marasinghe is Ariyaratne's daughter.
28. Zadek and Szabo, *Valuing Organisation.*
29. Zadek and Szabo, *Valuing Organisation*, 34.
30. Quoted in Wismeijer, *From Charisma to Bureaucracy?*, 62.

Part II

City Lights: The South

After centuries in the country, Everyman and Everywoman are moving into town. Every year, population distribution figures tilt a little further toward the cities as another 60 million urban babies are born and some 20 million immigrants stream in from the impoverished countryside.[1] Within fifteen years' time, the majority of the world's people will be city dwellers. *Homo sapiens* will have become an urban species.[2]

The urban boom is concentrated in the South. Fifty years ago, big cities were the North's problem—and a relatively small one at that. Only one in every hundred people lived in a city with over a million inhabitants.[3] These metropolises had time to adapt. It took Paris a century to grow from half a million to 3 million inhabitants,[4] and London 130 years to grow from 1 million to 8 million.[5]

By 1980, every tenth person on earth lived in a million-plus city,[6] and vast settlements were becoming a feature of the South. By 1990, twenty-seven of the world's forty largest cities were in developing countries, and they each had between 4 million and 21 million inhabitants.[7] Unlike Europe's capitals, these cities have not had the luxury of time: Mexico City's population soared from 1 million to 20 million in under 50 years.[8] Nearly three-quarters of Latin America's population and nearly a third of Asia's now live in cities.[9]

These huge communities put a crushing burden on their environment—and on their inhabitants. In 1985, half the world's urban population lived in areas where the air was dangerous to breathe, a quarter had no access to clean water, and two-fifths had no sanitation.[10] Too few have proper homes.

Poor city dwellers can rarely afford even subsidized housing or land on which to build. Researchers in Peru found that if a group of low-income families wanted to obtain a vacant lot, the seven years of negotiation involved would cost each person more than four years' earnings (at the minimum wage).[11] As a result, people make homes where they can: on the pavements of Calcutta and Bombay, in the shelters and burial vaults of a cemetery in Cairo, and in burrows in a garbage dump in Mexico City. Two-fifths of Latin America's city dwellers, a quarter of Asia's, and two-thirds of Africa's live in shantytowns—in shelters of cardboard, corrugated iron, wood, or brick built on land that does not belong to them.[12]

The problems are massive and often beyond the resources, let alone the will, of national and municipal authorities to resolve. In the late 1980s, only thirty-eight new houses were built in the South for every 100 families needing homes, and even these were way beyond the rent or mortgage range of their prospective inhabitants.[13] By contrast, squatters in Lima, Peru, had built over $8.3 billion worth of housing in the preceding two decades—forty-seven times the amount spent by the state on low-cost public housing.[14] In the past, urban authorities often discouraged self-help initiatives. The future, many experts believe, lies in their learning to assist them.

In 1992, I visited Rio de Janeiro, a pioneer in the South's urban and shanty explosion and in both government and grassroots responses to it. In the 1960s, cooperation between government and shanty community leaders led to an ambitious and, in the short term, successful rehousing program. That decade also saw the birth of a more enduring trend as communities came together to rebuild their homes and pressure the authorities into providing services and tenure. This do-it-yourself urbanization continues today. Both processes owe much to a spiritual revival that swept through the city's shantytowns in the 1960s. That story is told in Chapter 4.

The next two chapters touch on another aspect of urban existence: working life. They deal with a fortunate minority in many cities of the South: those with formal jobs. Chapter 5 tells the story of two taxi drivers' cooperatives in Rio de Janeiro that have improved working conditions and set out to fight the corruption that is undermining Brazil's economic and political life. Chapter 6 looks at a company in the Indian steel city of Jamshedpur that has found that investing in its employees' personal development is a key to industrial success.

Notes

1. Paul Harrison, *The Third Revolution: Population, Environment and a Sustainable World* (London: Penguin, 1993); Herbert Girardet, *The Gaia Atlas of Cities* (London: Gaia Books, 1992).
2. Geoffrey Lean and Don Hinrichson, *WWF Atlas of the Environment* (Oxford: Helicon, 1992).
3. Lean and Hinrichson, *WWF Atlas*.
4. Lester Brown and Jodi Jacobson, "Assessing the Future of Urbanization," in *State of the World 1987: Worldwatch Institute Report* (New York: W. W. Norton, 1987).
5. Lean and Hinrichson, *WWF Atlas*.
6. Lean and Hinrichson, *WWF Atlas*.
7. Girardet, *Gaia Atlas*.
8. Lean and Hinrichson, *WWF Atlas*.
9. UNDP, *Human Development Report, 1994* (New York/Oxford: Oxford University Press, 1994).
10. *UNEP Profile, 1990* (Nairobi: United Nations Environment Program, 1990).
11. Marcia D. Lowe, "Shaping Cities," in *State of the World 1992: Worldwatch Institute Report* (New York: W. W. Norton, 1992).
12. Harrison, *Third Revolution*.
13. Harrison, *Third Revolution*.
14. Lowe, "Shaping Cities."

CHAPTER 4

People Power in Rio's Favelas

A little hill rising above the old docks of Rio de Janeiro has given its name to the world's best-known urban problem. It was here, on the Morro da Favela, that the city's first shantytown appeared seventy years ago. Today Rio has 600 favelas, home to between 1.5 and 3 million people.

Every year, 300,000 people arrive in Rio, many of them fleeing drought and hunger in northeastern Brazil. They have little hope of finding affordable housing, so they build wherever they can find a space. Shacks scramble up the sides of Rio's precipitous hills and huddle over its marshy swamps. There are even homes wedged into the triangles where overpasses meet the ground.

The city's more comfortable inhabitants—known by the favela dwellers as "the people of the asphalt" because their streets are paved—fear and avoid the favelas. Rio is one of the world's most violent cities, with a murder rate three times New York's.[1] Its drug barons, based in the shantytowns, boast a business volume equal to that of McDonald's in Brazil—US$2.5 million a week.[2] Thousands of children hustle and mug on the city streets, escaping pursuit in the labyrinthine alleys of the favelas. Many die violently—some, it is believed, at the hands of the police.

Violence and crime are not the whole story of the favelas, however. These jumbles of brick, board, and tin are the site of one of the great human development stories of our time, dating back forty years to the founding of the first community associations. Many of the older hillside communities now look more like Mediterranean villages than slums, with brick houses, piped water, paved streets, electricity, sewerage, and rubbish collection. Their inhabitants owe these amenities not to the authorities but to their own resourcefulness—and to community leaders who refused to be bullied, bribed, or ignored.

In 1992, I spent two weeks visiting favelas in Rio de Janeiro with Luiz Pereira. In the 1960s, Pereira led a council of favelas representing 50,000 people. He was one of thousands of *favelados* who were rehoused in the 1960s and 1970s, thanks to a conjunction of international aid, government support, and grassroots initiative. Now retired, he devotes his energies to supporting his embattled successors in the favelas. This chapter tells the story of how Pereira and his contemporaries took charge of their own destiny and of how one community is following in their footsteps today.

Three factors converged in the early 1960s to improve the prospects of Rio's 1.25 million favela dwellers: finance, political will, and an upsurge of initiative in the communities themselves.

First, money became available. In 1961, concerned about Castro's ambitions outside Cuba, President John Kennedy led the United States and twenty-two Latin American countries in setting up the Alliance for Progress to counter communism by promoting democracy and development. The alliance was particularly keen to do what it could to avert revolution in Brazil, which was threatened by deep divisions between Left and Right, spiraling inflation, and repeated political crises. It offered support to Carlos Lacerda, a forceful right-winger who had become state governor for Rio de Janeiro and its hinterland in 1961.

Lacerda provided the second factor in the equation: government commitment to tackling Rio's housing problems. For this, he was able to draw on alliance funds. He made it known that his door would always be open for favela leaders—but they had to be elected by their communities. As a result, communities all over the city began to organize themselves into residents' associations.

Many of the first rehousing schemes were unpopular and unsuccessful, and the motives behind them were, of course, mixed. Some favelas occupied prime sites in the center of the city, which property developers were eager to buy. Communities were split up, and people were moved miles away from their jobs—sometimes to inadequate "temporary" housing that became permanent. Such settlements as Vila Kennedy, now a thriving satellite town outside Rio, were fiercely resented. The favelas themselves were deeply divided by political infighting and corruption. Absorbed in settling old scores and in feathering their own nests, their leaders were unable to present a united case to the authorities.

It was here that a third factor came into play—a spiritual revival among the *favelados*. That led to the growth of trust, integrity, and self-help initiatives. It came from an unexpected source: the docks of Rio, which a decade before had been paralyzed by unofficial strikes, gangs, union rivalries, and corruption.[3] Two leaders of rival unions made it their common cause to unite the port. They had been inspired by the ideas of Moral Re-Armament (MRA), an international network of people who saw spiritual change in individuals as an essential component of successful social change.

Over a period of years, the union leaders' campaign had a remarkable impact on their colleagues. Theft, corruption, and personal vendettas began to decline. Several couples returned to the church and got married, accompanied by their children. In 1957, the port held its first genuinely free union elections. By 1960, the new, united union had over 4,000 members—compared with the official union's 700 members in 1955—and there had not been a strike since 1954. If personal choices could have such dramatic results in their situation, the dockers asked, what about Rio's other major problem area—the favelas?

Among those who had been impressed by the dockers' experiences was industrialist Antônio Guedes Muniz, a close associate of Lacerda's. He and his wife invited some of the dockers to their home to meet José de Almeida Neto, an activist who lived in a local favela.[4]

De Almeida was astonished to be invited to a bourgeois home and even more astonished by the people he met there, among them an industrialist who had built up a successful business without giving or taking bribes. The dockers showed him a feature film they had made about their experiences. "I suddenly saw that we *favelados* were not just 1 million problems but 2 million hands, ready to solve these problems," he said later. He offered to arrange for the dockers to visit the favelas with their film.

De Almeida worked in a government printing press and used his contacts to lobby on behalf of the favelas. He became Lacerda's representative in the favelas and applied the principles he had learned through the dockers and their associates in his efforts to foster self-help in the communities. According to one source, 110 community associations were founded as a result.[5]

My guide to the favelas, Luiz Pereira, was one of those most dramatically affected by de Almeida's campaign. A tile fitter, he had come to Rio in 1952 with his wife, Edir, and five children. They came from Fortaleza in drought-stricken northeastern Brazil, hoping like so many others for a better life in the big city. At first, they lived in a shack across the bay from Rio, and Pereira had to leave at four each morning to catch the bus and ferry to work. Because the family had no clock, he once arrived at the ferry at 1 A.M., having mistaken the last bus of the night for the first of the morning. It was a relief to move into Rio, to the favela of Morro de São João.

Their shack had no running water or electricity, and Luiz had to build a fence to prevent the children from falling down the steep hill on which it was built. Edir took in washing, toiling up the hill in the hot sun with her tin of water. "People used to tell me to leave my husband and go home to Fortaleza," she says. "There are always people to tell you that you could have an easier life if you just let go of your principles."

"One day a man from the government said that we should not have to pay rent for our shacks," remembers Pereira. "So everyone stopped paying. It led to a storm for our people, because the landowners wanted us out." A wave of evictions hit the favelas. As the communities organized themselves informally for defense, Pereira found himself taking leadership of Morro de São João.

He speaks with feeling of the day the police came with tear gas and bayonets and tore down a third of the shacks on the hill. "Every family took someone in," says Pereira. "In our home you had to step over all the people sleeping on the floor. After that, many people didn't believe in the authorities anymore, or in a God who would allow over 200 people to lose their homes."

The evictions shocked the government into declaring a state of emergency, during which no houses could be demolished. With great daring, Pereira seized the respite to take his case to Lacerda and was rewarded with the promise of a visit from a state representative the next week. When Pereira set about formulating the community's demands, he had to be persuaded to add water and sanitation to the list. "I thought that would be asking for too much," he says.

The government representative urged the community to set up a legal association and to keep him abreast of their needs. Pereira was elected president by acclamation and went on to become president of a council of local favelas representing nearly 50,000 people. With his colleagues, he put up furious opposition to government plans to rehouse favela dwellers outside of town, up to a two-hour bus ride from their places of work.

Meanwhile, Edir was getting fed up. "Luiz got more and more accustomed to living in the favela and became very popular. He went to all the dances, but he refused to take me. I got very bitter." She had good reason to complain, acknowledges Luiz. "I didn't allow her to speak; I didn't let my children take part in anything; the directors in our community association had to do what I said. Wherever I spoke I was applauded, and the more I was applauded the more foolishnesses I said. I began to believe that everything I did was right."

As Pereira's influence grew, so did his feeling that the harder he worked, the poorer he became. His bitterness against those he considered responsible—the rich, the government, and the North Americans—increased. He was horrified when de Almeida and his MRA friends, some of them from overseas, climbed up

J. Henderson

Luiz and Edir Pereira: "it was we ourselves with the help of the state government"

to the favela. "I told him he was a sell-out, and that if he hadn't been there we'd have literally kicked the foreigners off the hill," says Pereira.

In spite of Pereira's attempts to discourage them, the MRA campaigners went on visiting him over a period of eighteen months. Eventually he began to see their point. "Some of the things they said made me think. I saw that bitterness and revolt would not build what I wanted in the community and in Brazil. A series of changes began in my life." He began to set aside time each morning to think and "listen to [his] inner voice." He made up with Edir and the family, adopted a more democratic approach in the association, and became reconciled with an enemy who had twice tried to kill him. "It's very important to have your head cleaned out, so you can think of fresh things," he explains.

As Pereira became less autocratic, others in the community began to get involved. Over the next months, the association—

reinforced by a newly founded women's wing—built stairs and ramps up the hill to replace the slippery mud paths, installed tanks and pumps for water distribution, and concreted in the huge boulders that threatened to roll down and crush their huts. "There was no lawyer getting this for us, it was we ourselves with the help of the state government," Pereira says proudly. When the people of the asphalt set up a three-member committee to beautify the neighborhood, Pereira had the chutzpah to put himself up for election and won a place on the committee.

With the threat of eviction still hanging over their heads, Pereira and his colleagues drew up a plan for building new apartments not far from Morro de São João. When they failed to get this plan implemented through a housing association, Pereira had the bright idea of telephoning the minister of the interior. "To my amazement, I got straight through to him and he asked me to come and see him," he says.

After lengthy negotiations, the apartments were built, and the community moved in 1970. When the Pereiras walked into their new home, Edir was so overcome by the sight of the bathroom and kitchen, with running water, that she cried.

Another favela leader who adopted a new style of leadership was Euclides da Silva, president of the community of Parada de Lucas.[6] He held the electricity concession for 526 homes in his favela and was making a tidy profit by buying power for four cruzeiros a kilowatt and selling it for eleven. His rival, Amfilófilo, held the concession for another part of the favela, and the two men had made frequent attempts on each other's lives. The community was deeply divided.

When the dockers came to show their film at Parada de Lucas, da Silva stayed to talk with them. "They told us about the difference it had made in their lives when they began to live by absolute standards of honesty, purity, unselfishness, and love," he recalled later. "They struck me as being effective and fearless. They came to see me many times. Finally I took an honest look at my own life. I thought of my wife, of Amfilófilo, whom I had tried to kill, and how I was cheating the people over electricity. I had a struggle within myself, a fight between my greed and ambition and what God wanted from me. I knew I had to clean up my life—and I knew where I had to start. It wasn't easy."

Da Silva had a "heart-to-heart talk" with his wife, to whom he had been frequently and openly unfaithful, and they rebuilt their marriage. After several aborted attempts, he approached Amfilófilo, and the two men reached an understanding. He told his customers that he had been overcharging them and resigned his position as president, only to be reelected. People in the favela began to trust him—and one another.

Da Silva was elected president of a federation of 60,000 *favelados* and took part in the dockers' campaign to show their film in each of the city's 186 favelas. Busloads of favela leaders drove up to the MRA center at Petropolis, an hour and a half from Rio, to recharge their batteries and discuss their problems away from the turmoil of the city, in an atmosphere where they were encouraged to examine their own motives and values.

The relationships built there made it possible for a group of favela presidents to take a united proposal on rehousing to Lacerda and the state authorities. According to da Silva, speaking in 1967, this led to new homes or better conditions for 500,000 people, funded by an Alliance for Progress grant and the state budget. More than 5,000 homes were rebuilt by their inhabitants on the sites where the shacks used to be, using materials provided by the state.

In the 1950s, da Silva had been involved in one of the less successful rehousing projects arranged by the Catholic Church's Cruzada São Sebastião. Over 700 people had been rehoused in apartments, but the community had disintegrated into crime and lawlessness. Da Silva believed that the chaos of his own private life had contributed to the project's failure and that his new honesty was part of the later scheme's success.[7]

Lacerda's government set up a Company for Popular Housing to spearhead its rehousing campaign. Its first president, Sandra Cavalcânti (later a member of the federal legislature) made a point of consulting a general committee of favela leaders, which included da Silva and de Almeida, before making any decisions.

"We wanted to be sure that our projects answered the most urgent needs," she explained. "The change in the attitude of the favela leaders made this collaboration very fruitful. We were able to prepare people for their new surroundings."[8]

After a military government seized power in Brazil in 1964, it implemented the rehousing policies pioneered in Rio on a national basis. It set up a National Housing Bank, financed by a workers' insurance scheme, and by 1976, it had built over 600,000 units of low-income housing. The bank reckoned that the stimulus its work had given to the building industry indirectly produced another 2.5 million homes. By the early 1970s, the building industry was creating 500,000 new jobs a year. The whole development was one of the key factors in Brazil's economic miracle.[9]

The achievements of the National Housing Bank were impressive, but the poorest inhabitants of the favelas were unable to afford even the lowest rates of repayment. And in the long term, as in the rest of the developing world, the ambitious housing schemes of the 1960s proved too pricey to sustain. Although the population of Rio's favelas fell for a while, today, Morro de São João is covered with shacks once again, and Rio's favelas keep on growing.

Luiz Pereira looks back to the 1960s with something approaching nostalgia. "We did not like Carlos Lacerda," he says, "but when he started to build thousands of houses we changed our minds. Today there are no removals, but there is no building either."

More than ever, today's favela communities are having to rely on their own resources. The growth of the drug mafia has made favela politics even more dangerous than they were in Pereira's day. "There is a ghost of fear," said one of those I met. "If you speak out, you may be dead tomorrow." In these circumstances, the wise do what they can for their communities and keep out of the drug barons' hair—"each monkey on his own branch," as one community leader put it dryly. The fear is so pervasive that I was asked not to attribute these quotations.

In spite of this, all over Rio, the spirit of self-help lives on. At its heart are people of integrity, many of whom derive their strength from their faith and from the support of veterans like Pereira. The efforts of the community association of Nova Holanda are just one example.

When Lacerda's government cleared the favelas from south Rio's fashionable beach area in 1960, the poorest inhabitants were billeted in duplex huts in a marshy area called the Maré until they could afford to move on to proper housing. For most of them, that day never came. Thirty years later, some 240,000 people live in Nova Holanda and the other eleven communities of the Maré.

For the people transplanted in 1960, the twelve-mile move was traumatic. José Carlos de Souza was nineteen. He had a job near the favela where he grew up and had been training with a local football team. "My whole life was organized around that part of the city," he says. "With the move, our community exploded. Everyone was sent to different places. Only the strongest survived." For the next fifteen years, he had a serious alcohol problem. "I was hypertense, depressed, and isolated, desperately afraid of dying. Even in a crowded football stadium, I was alone."

Eleven years ago, a month after his marriage, José Carlos found the willpower to stop drinking. "I had kept saying I would stop, but I had to discover the need to," he says. "I had to see myself in the mirror—only God could show me my reality. A few days after I stopped drinking, I found I could look people in the eyes for the first time." He became involved in community affairs and admits that, because he is so busy, his family has seen only a 70 percent improvement in him.

His colleague in Nova Holanda's community association, Ana Inés Sousa, left Paraíba in northeastern Brazil in 1970 when she was eight. "My father had a business and a little restaurant, but when drought hit the area, people had no money to spend. My father sold everything, went to Rio, and, when he had raised enough money to buy a small shack in Nova Holanda, he sent for us." She remembers her mother frantically trying to wash all six children each time the bus stopped on the forty-eight-hour journey.

For an eight-year-old used to a relatively comfortable life, Nova Holanda was a shock. "Everything was cramped," she remembers. "Near our home there was an open drain and one or two pigs. The smell was terrible. There was nothing: no social services, no water, no drainage, a lot of disease, crime, and violence." These conditions led her to become a nurse. When we met, she was lecturing in public health at Rio's Federal University. She could have afforded to move out of the favela, "but I can't even imagine how I would live in another place," she says.

Her family, devout Catholics, became involved in community work, running a church youth group that tried to keep children off the streets. "We succeeded in rehabilitating some of the youngsters who used to go to the tourist beaches and steal, but others were intimidated by their gangs or even killed."

Twelve years ago, Nova Holanda was a collection of duplex huts and wooden shacks, many of them on stilts over the marsh. Toddlers would fall into the water and drown. The community had an association, but its officers were government appointees who, says José Carlos, "regarded the state as their father." In 1984, the community held its first direct elections for the association. Ana Inés's sister, Eliana, was elected. "From then on the election process itself played a role of motivation and mobilization of the people," says José Carlos. In 1991, he took over the presidency from Ana Inés, who had succeeded Eliana in 1987.

At its first assembly in 1984, the community set its priorities: sanitation, water, paving, lighting, house repairs, a leisure area, a day nursery, a nonconventional school, and rubbish collection. The city authorities, used to presiding over an acquiescent community, suddenly found themselves bombarded with demands. Today, many of them have been achieved, although "much more was done by the community than by the government," asserts Ana Inés.

The association's flagship is its building cooperative and brickworks, shared with five neighboring associations. In 1988, the federal government asked the community to nominate families

M. Lean

José Carlos de Souza of Nova Holanda: "the priorities were defined by the people"

to receive 10,000-cruzeiro "reconstruction tickets" (worth about US$50 at the time)—not even enough to pay for a new door, according to Ana Inés.

"We called the community together and proposed that the tickets be pooled to form the initial capital of the co-op, with fewer families benefiting, so each could buy more," says José Carlos. "Everyone agreed—but then the problem was choosing the sixty families." The criteria were proximity to the co-op, willingness to work together, and some degree of building expertise. In the first year, seventy-three houses were built.

The co-op survived on this money until August 1989, buying materials in bulk and reselling them. Then, with the help of a grant from the Caixa Economica Federal, it set up its own brickworks. The brickworks and the building projects provide much-needed jobs for local people.

When I visited Nova Holanda one afternoon early in 1992, everybody seemed to be building. "That's Nova Holanda today," said Ana Inés proudly. Some 400 houses had been built since 1988, forty-six of them with government financing, co-op bricks, and community labor. The rest were built by individuals who bought their materials from the co-op.

The next concern is to find projects that will keep young people off the streets and give them an alternative to drugs. The association provides day care for toddlers whose mothers go out to work and arranges sports and other activities for older children and teenagers. It plans to set up a bakery to provide vocational training but is having difficulty finding the funds, in spite of sending out many project proposals. Any outside help comes from personal contacts made with foreign visitors.

The key to the association's success has been community involvement, according to José Carlos. "The priorities here were defined by the people—and because of this, they were motivated. If you feel you know best, people either feel offended or as if you are giving them a Christmas present. Other places have not advanced in the same way because the leaders didn't reach the people."

Another strength has been the continuity and integrity of Nova Holanda's leadership, who receive no pay. "Honesty, unity, and participation are key to running a cooperative," says Ana Inés. "It won't work if people pocket the money." Although at the time of my visit she was no longer president, the association took up most of her spare time. "I work all day and then come home to a meeting until 11 P.M. People don't worry if it's early in the morning or late at night; if they have a blocked drain or their lights don't work or they need a nurse, they come to me. You can hang your private life on a nail. But if nobody had that kind of love for the community, few advances would happen."

The shanties and slums of the South are the world's fastest growing communities. They show amazing resourcefulness in the face of crushing odds. Today, most new housing in developing countries is built by its inhabitants—for a fifth of the cost of equivalent public housing.[10] Some enlightened city governments have backed these initiatives, but such schemes are rare, and an estimated 70 to 95 percent of new urban housing in the South is still unauthorized.[11]

As the experiences of Pereira, da Silva, José Carlos, and Ana Inés demonstrate, spiritual conviction can be a powerful element in the struggle for better conditions. Forty-three-year-old Danilo Ferreira de Souza, who has presided over the transformation of the favela of Morro dos Cabritos, puts it this way: "I was born and brought up here. I have carried many cans of water. I have cut trees for fuel, killed birds for food, picked up leftovers in the street market. I have seen people die of hepatitis, meningitis, and TB or be killed by bandits or police. We are not different from everyone else; we are the same people. I couldn't understand why there was so much discrimination." He adds, "I have a childish dream that the world can change. I know now that this may not be true, but the dream stays with me."

All over Rio and the South, shanty dwellers go on working as if this dream could come true. The hope for the world's cities lies in governments taking them seriously.

Notes

I visited Rio de Janeiro in February 1992 to research an article on the favelas for *For a Change* (August/September 1992). Unless otherwise stated, this chapter is based on my interviews and encounters then and at international conferences since. I am grateful to all those who received me in their communities; to Luis and Evelyn Puig, Laurie and Elsa Vogel, Erwin Zimmerman, Daniel Puig, Ademar Broutelles, and David Howell for translating and for their insights; and to Luiz Pereira for introducing me to his colleagues.

1. Herbert Girardet, *The Gaia Atlas of Cities* (London: Gaia Books, 1992).
2. *Jornal do Brasil*, February 16, 1992.
3. Gabriel Marcel, *Fresh Hope for the World* (London: Longmans, Green and Co., 1960).
4. *Build on Solid Ground* (slide and tape production, Associação Brasileira para o Rearmamento Moral, 1975).
5. *New World News*, July 12, 1975.
6. Euclides da Silva died in 1979. His story is drawn from his own accounts in *Build on Solid Ground*, in the *MRA Information Service* of February 25, 1967, and in *O Caminho Certo*, published as a special supplement to *Diario de Noticias*, Rio de Janeiro, in 1965.
7. Charles Piguet and Michel Sentis, *The World at the Turning* (London: Grosvenor Books, 1982).

8. *Build on Solid Ground.*
9. Geoffrey Lean, *Rich World, Poor World* (London: George Allen and Unwin, 1978).
10. Girardet, *Gaia Atlas.*
11. Marcia Lowe, "Shaping Cities," in *State of the World 1992: Worldwatch Institute Report* (New York: W. W. Norton, 1992).

CHAPTER 5

Rio's Honest Taxi Drivers

Tax evasion robs the British government of an estimated US$15 billion every year. The situation is even graver in Greece, Italy, Portugal, and Spain, whose informal economies are thought to equal between 20 and 30 percent of their gross domestic products.[1] In the last decade, high-level corruption has toppled governments from Italy to Japan, from Brazil to the Philippines; African leaders are thought to have amassed over US$20 billion in Swiss bank accounts.[2] By the end of 1987, citizens of the fifteen developing countries with the largest foreign debts had stashed away up to US$300 billion overseas—over half what their countries owed.[3]

All over the world and at all levels of society, corruption eats away at national development. It is the fault line where private morality threatens public security. It exacerbates the gulf between rich and poor, giving "a free unseen pay rise to people already earning many times the poor man's income," in the words of development writer Paul Harrison.[4] It warps official decision making on projects, purchases, and personnel: "the soundness of judgement is inevitably in inverse ratio to the number of dollars flowing into personal coffers as a result of the exercise of that judgement," comments George Moody-Stuart of Transparency International.[5] And it undermines economies: "at the root of Brazil's inflation problem is the determination of rich and middle-class Brazilians not to pay taxes," wrote *Observer* correspondent Hugh O'Shaughnessy on February 7, 1993, when the country's inflation was 30 percent.

In countries where everyone is on the take, some question whether it is possible for the average person to be honest and survive. An answer comes from a notoriously dishonest profession in a country racked by corruption scandals. Taxi drivers in Rio de Janeiro are discovering that if they work together, honesty not only is possible but also makes good business sense.

Every newcomer to Rio de Janeiro is warned about the risks of hailing one of the city's 22,000 yellow cabs. The driver may take exotic detours, tamper with the meter, fail to show passengers the conversion table that translates the meter reading into a fare, or even mug or rob them. In 1990, Brazil's association of travel agents was so concerned about the problem and its effect on tourism that it called a meeting with taxi drivers' leaders.

Fifteen years ago, Rio's cabbies were regarded as the worst on the continent, maintains José Batista Filho, a founding member of two taxi cooperatives that are changing the profession's image. "Our cabs were old and badly maintained; drivers were bad-tempered and bitter, with little idea of their rights and responsibilities. Quite a number cheated or threatened their passengers. We were regarded as hopeless cases."

Most drivers rented their cars at extortionate rates from rapacious owners. Without insurance, any accident or breakdown was an economic catastrophe. And the profession's reputation for dishonesty was bad for business. "Clients did not trust us," says Batista Filho. "You could drive around the city all day without picking up enough fares to pay for the petrol."

Today, things are different. Rio has at least fourteen taxi cooperatives and associations, transporting some 5 million people a year. Their members have the security of car ownership and insurance, as well as regular work through phone bookings and contracts. "Our taxis are the latest models and well-maintained," Batista Filho asserts. Because the first cooperatives insisted on a code of honesty, other groups of drivers have been forced to follow suit—including those attached to the airports. Soon, he reckons, people will be able to take cabs in Rio without fear of being taken for a ride.

For Rio's cabbies, one name sums up the cooperative movement—Americo Martorelli. This charismatic Italian immigrant was the inspiration behind the city's first successful yellow-cab cooperatives, Central de Taxi and Coopataxi. He was on the board of one or other until his sudden death in 1991. The key to the two co-ops' success, say their present directors, was Martorelli's passion for integrity. According to his widow, Carmella, this resulted from a turnaround in his life that had dramatic effects at home.

Americo and Carmella had gone to the same school in Italy but met only after they arrived in Brazil, he in 1948 and she in 1950. Within eight months, they had married. "He was serving coffee at the Ambassador Hotel, I was working in an office," she remembers. "We adored each other." They had three daughters and a son.

The idyll did not last. "I woke up to the fact that he was drinking, smoking, and gambling hard," says Carmella. "We had no more peace and no more money. We were short of everything. He was terribly jealous: he'd even be jealous of his own shadow if it came too near to me." He was violent with the children. "This went on for seventeen years. The children told me I ought to throw him out. But he didn't want to leave us." And as a Catholic, she says, "I thought it would be a sin to separate."

In 1972, after a number of other ventures, Martorelli rented a car and began to work as a taxi driver. He was outraged by the way the drivers were exploited by the car owners, and in 1976, he got involved with an attempt to set up a cooperative[6]. The drivers were so disunited, however, that there seemed little hope of its getting off the ground. Someone invited a group from Moral Re-Armament (MRA) to attend a meeting, in the hopes of encouraging a rapprochement.

One of the MRA visitors, Luis Puig, remembers a "slightly drunk-seeming" Martorelli listening quietly while different

speakers described how they had made a new start in their lives
and then announcing, loudly, that he did not understand what
they were talking about. Someone described solidarity as meaning that when someone else has a hole in his shoe, your foot feels
cold. "Ah," said Martorelli, "I see the point."

Afterwards, Puig and Martorelli found themselves waiting
together at the bus stop. Martorelli began to talk about his life.
"Bus after bus went by, but I didn't want to interrupt him," Puig
recalls. Eventually, Martorelli asked, "What shall I do? I feel des-
perate. I have hurt my wife and my children. I lead a very dis-
orderly life." The only thing Puig could think of saying was,
"God has a plan for you." Martorelli thought for a long moment
and then he said, "Is that true?" When he got onto the bus he
was smiling.

Martorelli went home, woke Carmella, and announced
that he was a changed man. Understandably annoyed at being
awoken at 2 A.M., she didn't believe a word of it, particularly as
his explanation was that he had met some wonderful friends. "I
thought they'd be like the other friends he'd brought home—
no good," she says.

Americo took Carmella to meet Puig and his colleagues. For
Carmella, they represented a kind of hope. "I had lost my faith
so much," she says, "but these were people I could trust. It was
so different from what we had at home."

One morning, Martorelli informed Carmella that he was
giving up alcohol. She was used to such promises, so she was
astonished when he actually did it. Then he gave up smoking
just as suddenly—an extraordinary achievement for a five-pack-
a-day man. One day, according to Puig, Martorelli was driving
and began coughing so badly that he had to pull over to the side
of the road. He threw his pack of cigarettes out the window and
told his passenger that he was giving up smoking for good. The
passenger, who turned out to be a lung specialist, told him that
he was doing the right thing—and offered him a prize if he kept
it up for a month. Martorelli never smoked again. When the
specialist praised his willpower, Martorelli responded, "It's not
willpower, it's God."

Americo Martorelli (left), the inspiration behind Rio de Janeiro's first successful yellow cab cooperative

Meanwhile, the taxi cooperative that had been launched at the meeting was experiencing hard times. In an attempt to ensure integrity, its founders had included a commitment to absolute standards of morality among its bylaws but had failed to translate this statement into practice. Before long, the co-op collapsed because of corruption and authoritarianism. A second attempt failed to get off the ground when Martorelli and his colleagues realized that it was geared to promoting a local politician.

Fired by the changes in his personal life, Martorelli was undaunted. "I can't understand why these co-ops shouldn't work," he told Puig. "I will enlist the men I trust." Central de Taxi, founded in 1977, resurrected the bylaws of the first cooperative and nearly twenty years later still describes itself proudly as a "working cooperative . . . with absolute standards" (*Cooperativa de trabalho em taxi e transportes com padroes absolutas*).

The early meetings were stormy. The issue of whether to pay bribes to secure contracts was particularly contentious. One day

Martorelli telephoned Puig and announced with characteristic drama, "I have defeated dishonesty." He had had an accident, and the owner of his car had agreed to pay for the repairs. The garage mechanic offered to double his estimate so that Martorelli could pocket the difference. When Martorelli refused on the grounds that the country had enough crooks already, the mechanic was outraged. Martorelli used the experience to convince his colleagues in the co-op to accept his no-bribes policy.

Martorelli had stopped drinking, smoking, and gambling; he was striving to be honest at work and no longer reached for his iron bar when he was abused by fellow drivers in the heat of Rio's rush hour. But things were still difficult at home. Eventually, some years after their first meeting with Puig, the Martorellis turned to him for advice. He suggested that it might help if Americo and Carmella allowed themselves the space and silence to review their lives and ask God what he wanted them to do, and then compared notes with each other. Sitting side by side on one of Rio's beaches, they found the courage to tell each other things they had always kept hidden. Afterwards, they sat for nearly half an hour without saying a word. Then, for the first time in years, they went to the movies together.

Carmella couldn't believe that the harmony would last—but it did. "I'm not saying we became angels, but we never had the sort of fights we had before," she says. Their twelve-year-old son, Vincente, who had had convulsions since he was three, began to get better. Today, like his father before him, he drives a yellow cab.

Martorelli's two cooperatives, Central de Taxi and Coopataxi (founded in 1979), aimed to win a better deal for both drivers and passengers. Initially, each co-op served a separate purpose. Coopataxi was a consumers' cooperative, offering drivers the chance to buy cars, fuel, and repairs at low prices. Central de Taxi set up a radio cab service and business contracts, which gave its drivers greater job security. A driver could be a member of both co-ops.

Legal changes in 1988 meant that drivers could belong to only one cooperative. Coopataxi set up its own radio system and

kept its service facilities open to all Rio's drivers. Its member-
ship dropped from 800 to 250, believed to be the maximum
possible for efficiency. "A co-op is like a small blanket," says Paulo
César da Silva Campos, president in 1992 of Central de Taxi,
which had 258 drivers. "If you have too many members, there
isn't enough work to go around."

Both cooperatives have stringent enrollment procedures.
Prospective members must prove that both they and their ve-
hicles have clean records. In the case of Central de Taxi, drivers
must submit to a lecture on their obligations from the executive
directors' board. The entry fee and subscriptions cover insurance. Drivers are policed by a council of ethics and discipline
made up of their peers. "If a client is badly treated, he or she
can phone us and make a complaint," says Manuel Antônio Pena
Neto, president of Coopataxi in 1992. "The driver may then be
warned, suspended, or dismissed." The bylaws of Central de Taxi
cite overcharging as an offense punishable by ejection from the
co-op. And, true to Martorelli's early insistence, neither cooperative pays bribes.

This strictness pays dividends. Clients choose the taxis they
can trust: Central de Taxi receives nearly 40,000 calls a month.
"We have grown out of the dishonesty of others," says one of its
directors, Lúcio Malheiros de Carvalho, with satisfaction. His
own career is evidence that the strictness goes along with a belief
in rehabilitation: "Before I got into Central de Taxi, I used to
slash the tires of the cars of its members. Now I'm a director of
the co-op."

The system has to protect the driver as well as the passenger.
"Robbing a cabbie is like taking sweets from a child," says Pena
Neto. "You have to pick up whoever hails you. I've been robbed
three times. In most cases where drivers have resisted, they have
been killed." A driver's wife admits that she prays for her husband's safety every day: "He's going into the street, and who
knows who he's going to take into his taxi. I'm always relieved
when he gets home."

Although co-op drivers can still be hailed on the street, much
of their work involves responding to phone orders, relayed by

radio from headquarters. When a client calls to order a taxi, the operator takes the number and calls the client back to confirm that the car is on its way—and that the caller is bona fide. In the first four years of using its radio system, Coopataxi had no cases of robbery following phone orders.

"Martorelli did for us what even a government minister could not do," says Batista Filho. "He organized what was not organized. He aimed to create not just structures, but people who had a serious intention to serve the public. When we launched our cooperative, our aim was to provide the city with better services, to improve working conditions for drivers, and to improve economic conditions for their families." In spite of Brazil's spiraling economic crisis, these aims have all been achieved—not, however, without a struggle.

In 1988, when Coopataxi became a working cooperative, it plunged into an administrative crisis. "The directors were not ready for the tremendous financial leap involved," says Mauro Pereira de Souza, who was called in at that time. "The crisis at the co-op coincided with the economic crisis in Brazil. Inflation was soaring, and money lost its value overnight. Members were taking advantage, refusing to pay their fees." He and a colleague who had once worked in a bank, Delfín Ribeiro Pinto, set about restructuring the co-op.

In their attempt to reassert the directors' authority and to balance the books, de Souza and Pinto made enemies, and a power struggle ensued. They resigned in April 1989, were reelected (as president and treasurer, with Martorelli as vice president) in March 1990, and were voted out again in March 1991. The new board hauled de Souza and Pinto up on spurious charges and suspended them for a fortnight, against the wishes of the council of ethics.

"This created something you could really call hatred inside me," says de Souza. "My heart was completely closed against these people. Americo [who had also been ousted] kept asking me to forget this bitterness, but I felt my reasons were stronger." Eventually, during a weekend conference organized by MRA, he told Martorelli that he was "finished with the hatred" and, on his return to Rio, made the rounds of the directors, burying the hatchet.

A few days later, Martorelli had a fatal stroke. Two hundred taxi drivers attended his funeral, including both factions from Coopataxi. The reconciliation enabled de Souza and Pinto, though no longer officeholders in the co-op, to continue to promote its values.

Since Martorelli's death, Mauro Pereira de Souza, Delfín Ribeiro Pinto and José Batista Filho have taken up his mantle. Their aim is not just to spread an ethos of honesty among Rio's cabbies but to challenge corruption throughout society. For instance, before the 1994 elections, they took part in a national campaign for "clean elections."

They have been joined by Reginaldo de Souza, a former street child (and no relation to Mauro), who recently founded a third co-op with an explicit commitment to honesty. He started to live on the streets when he was ten, after his father killed his mother in a drunken rage. By the age of fourteen, he was taking drugs and stealing to pay for them; at seventeen, he was managing a drug outlet and living in fear of his life.

When Reginaldo was fifteen, a family of evangelical Christians befriended him. They helped him get an identity card, a process that took two years. He refused to live with them because, he says, "I wouldn't have felt free to go on doing what I was doing." But eventually, at the age of nineteen, he was able to listen to their advice. He had lost his interest in religion when he lost his parents, but he began to return to his faith. "It was not a quick change," he says, "but I never returned to drugs or crime."

In 1978, Reginaldo moved into the favela of Joaquim Meier, then only eight wooden shacks on land belonging to the government. He had just finished the ground floor of his house—and used up all his money—when the military police came and tore it down, along with the unfinished homes of five other new arrivals. They did not touch the houses that had been completed. As soon as the police left, Reginaldo and his neighbors got together and began to rebuild their houses cooperatively, racing to get the roofs on before the police returned. "When they came back, they found me in my house—even though it was only one room, with no windows—and they left me alone."

The community set up an association that persuaded the city to provide water, light, sewerage, and some asphalting. Under Reginaldo's leadership, the community gained ownership of the land and rebuilt their houses in brick. He started football teams, a youth federation, and a choir to keep the children off the streets. It has been a struggle to keep things going in recent years, and some of his projects have foundered for lack of people to carry them on. "Our life isn't marvelous," he says. "But solutions don't come in one hour, quickly. Someone has to take the first step."

The philosophy behind Reginaldo's taxi cooperative is simple: "If I overcharge, say a doctor, he may then overcharge his patient, say a storekeeper, who will in turn raise prices in his store. And I may be the customer."[7]

The experience of Rio's honest taxi drivers shows that even in a society where corruption is endemic, it is possible for individuals to be straight. When Americo Martorelli first started putting his principles into practice, it would have been understandable for Carmella to worry about the family finances. Americo sought out a client who had overpaid him and returned the money, he refused to increase his fares during a bus strike, and, when he began to work full time for the co-ops, he rented his car to another driver at a fair rate. "In spite of all this, our finances went all right," said Carmella. "It was very interesting."

The secret of the success of the cooperatives is, of course, that they work together. What their drivers lose in individual fares by being honest they get back in the increased business provided by the co-op's radio facilities and reputation, in cheaper services, and in the security of insurance. The incentive for the drivers is the better working conditions rather than the honesty—but the honesty is what has made the cooperatives so successful that other taxi drivers are following their example.

What was needed was for someone to have the courage to start. For Martorelli, that courage was raised by his personal

P. Carr

Carmella Martorelli: finances worked in spite of honesty

rebirth: the belief that God had a purpose for his life and the discovery that he could become free from his addictions and rebuild his home life. He not only administered the cooperatives, he nurtured their souls and believed that they had something to offer Brazil as a whole. His successors, fired by their own spiritual growth, share this determination.

Notes

This chapter is based on interviews in February 1992 with Carmella Martorelli, Paulo César da Silva Campos, Manuel Antônio Pena Neto, José Batista Filho, Lúcio Malheiros de Carvalho, Mauro Pereira de Souza, Delfín Ribeiro Pinto, and Reginaldo de Souza and on more recent correspondence and interviews with Luis and Evelyn Puig. Thanks once again to the Puigs, Laurie and Elsa Vogel, Daniel Puig, and Ademar Broutelles for translating and for their insights.

1. *The Economist*, August 14, 1993.
2. George Moody-Stuart, *Grand Corruption in Third World Development* (privately published in Britain, 1993).
3. Patricia Adams, *Odious Debts* (London: Earthscan Publications, 1991).
4. Paul Harrison, *Inside the Third World* (London: Penguin Books, 1979), 369.
5. Moody-Stuart, *Grand Corruption*, 27.
6. Evelyn Puig, *New World News*, November 6, 1976.
7. Michael Henderson, *For a Change*, October 1990.

CHAPTER 6

Human Development
in India's Steel City

L ike Brazil, India is one of the industrial giants of
the developing world—in spite of the absolute pov-
erty that besets some two-fifths of its people.[1] Their future depends on social reform, more enlightened government spending,
a fairer international economic order, and grassroots initiatives—
but also on economic development, built on efficient industries.

In countries where capital investment is hard to raise, the key to
industrial progress is the workforce, believes Sarosh Ghandy, resi-
dent director of one of the world's largest truck manufacturers,
based in the northeastern state of Bihar. His firm, Tata Engineering
and Locomotive Company (Telco), makes three-quarters of the
trucks on India's roads and has exported to some sixty countries.[2]
Each truck that leaves its plant in Jamshedpur is said to create after-
sales employment for thirteen people. Telco ranks among India's
top five private-sector companies in terms of business volume.

Productivity and quality are the two vital components for
competing in the global market, according to Ghandy, and these
depend on "the involvement of our people." Because Telco has
poured investment into a state-of-the-art car factory in Pune on
the other side of India, it has been unable to modernize its plant
in Jamshedpur. "We have to make up in 'software' where we are
lacking in hardware. We are building on the skills, commitment,
and involvement of our people."

The company has focused its human resources development
efforts in an innovative training program, launched in 1982.
Today the program saves the company millions of rupees every

year, has transformed relations between management and workers, and has improved conditions in the wider community beyond the factory gates. In August 1993, Britain's *Financial Times* described it as "a peculiarly Indian approach to quality and worker participation in a nation that has to contend with issues—from communal tensions to the effects of country liquor—not always on the agenda of western boardrooms." It was born out of the initiatives of a young trainee during a period of violent unrest in the plant's melting shop.

Telco belongs to the House of Tata, a vast industrial empire that includes Tata Steel (Tisco) and a wide range of other concerns from textiles to computers, chemicals to cosmetics, hydroelectric power to hotels. The group was founded in the nineteenth century by a devout Parsi, Jamsetji Tata, who believed that steel, hydroelectric power, and training were the key to India's industrial development. His successors built the city of Jamshedpur around the Tisco steelworks—India's first. It was the birthplace of the country's industrial revolution. Tata companies still employ members of over half the families there.[3]

Tata's has a tradition of concern for its workers, linked to the Parsi emphasis on doing good. Tisco pioneered the eight-hour work day, free medical care, works committees, insurance, training, and profit sharing long before they were legally required in European countries, let alone India.[4] Tisco has been free of strikes for over sixty years. Its sister companies share the group's commitment to training and welfare, although their industrial relations have not always been so harmonious.

In November 1972, when Kiran Gandhi joined Telco in Jamshedpur as a young engineering trainee, feelings were running high. The company had been paralyzed by a forty-eight-day strike in 1969. "There was a lot of anger because of the way the company's paternalism was being exploited," he says. "The troublemakers were being appeased and given benefits by management at the expense of others."

Gandhi was assigned to the melting shop of Telco's foundry. During his first year, there were five work stoppages of one to three days, caused by rivalry between the official union representative, V. N. Prasad, and a more radical group whose leaders included C. P. Singh. Workers were carrying knives and guns, and the police had to be called in when fighting broke out on the night shift. The management was considering shifting production from Jamshedpur to a new plant at Pune.

Gandhi was the son of a top executive at another Tata company and had planned to set up his own enterprise after graduating with honors from the Indian Institute of Technology near Bombay. But during his last year there, he had been deeply influenced by Moral Re-Armament (MRA) and had changed his plans. He believed that his conscience was telling him to do something about the industries that already existed rather than start a new one. "I felt national wealth was being wasted," he says. "One of the most important things I could do was to give the ideas of responsibility, teamwork, honesty, and change to Indian industry." He had adopted a daily practice of quiet reflection: "listening to the inner voice and acting upon it in faith." Now, faced with the unrest in his new place of work, he decided to get to know the protagonists.

"I was adding coke to the electrical furnace when I saw a young man with a notebook watching me," remembers V. N. Prasad. One of the undercurrents in the conflict was the fact that Prasad belonged to a lower caste than his opponents. His first impression of Gandhi was that "he belonged to a high-society family and came from a different world from mine." He was surprised to discover that Gandhi did not spend his evenings in the clubs and was even more surprised to be invited to his home and offered snacks by his mother. "Then he visited my wife and children and he became very close to me. This helped me not to hide anything in my heart." Prasad began to think again about his political opponents.

Gandhi also approached C. P. Singh. They found a common interest in the role of industry in India's development. When Singh expressed his concern about wastage of materials in the melting shop, Gandhi apologized to him for the prejudice that had made him think that workers just wanted more and more money for less and less work.

In March 1974, Singh's wife died in a smallpox epidemic. Gandhi took meals cooked by his mother to Singh's five small children. "It was the beginning of a lifelong friendship," says Singh. He was impressed by Gandhi's integrity—particularly by the fact that he had owned up to stealing from his college labs and had made restitution. "Until we met, I thought change could only be brought about by pressure and shouting. It had never occurred to me that it could be brought about by dialogue and listening."

Gandhi invited Prasad and Singh and some of their colleagues to MRA events in Jamshedpur and then to an international seminar at the MRA center in Maharashtra, Asia Plateau. The seminar encouraged participants to examine the link between their personal lives and the situations in their workplaces and to heed the dictates of conscience. "We met men who had decided to become honest with their wives, and capitalists who had decided not to evade taxes and to put people before profits," Prasad and Singh wrote in the Telco house magazine. Each found himself reassessing his attitude toward the other. Eventually, they both apologized and had a heart-to-heart talk. They decided to put aside their differences and to work together for the good of the country.

One slogan in particular stuck with Singh: "not who is right, but what is right." When his group called a new strike on his return, he refused to back it and supported Prasad, in spite of a death threat. After six months of day-to-day struggle by the two men, the rival groups were reconciled.

The spin-off for the company was considerable. The melting shop met its year's production target in ten months, leaving two months for maintenance work. When Prasad was promoted to supervisor, Singh took over his job as union representative. The melting shop has not had a work stoppage since. "It's not that we promised never to strike," says Singh, "but only to strike as a last resort."

The management, presented with this turnaround, was quick to recognize the benefit of Asia Plateau's approach and began to send groups of managers, union leaders, and workers to industrial seminars there. "The unique feature of those seminars is that managers and workers participate and live together," writes Chandreshwar Khan, assistant manager of Telco's Management Training Center.[5] Over the years, up to 500 Telco employees have attended, and many have returned with a new attitude toward their work, their family, and their colleagues.

In 1978, Telco's delegation consisted of four senior executives and four trade unionists. Among them was P. N. Pandey, a manager known for his tough, aggressive approach. His conscience was touched, he says, by "the philosophy of care for people." One of his first actions on his return was to apologize to a supervisor he had insulted twelve years before and had not spoken to since. The supervisor was completely overwhelmed: "He grabbed me in a hug. Tears were pouring down his face." Pandey's peers were astonished by the change in him, as were the workers, who now found that he offered them a chair when they visited his office.

Pandey also took note of the seminar's stress on absolute honesty as an antidote to corruption. He had taken a loan from the company on the pretext of buying a car and had produced false papers to back up his claim, although he had used the money for something else. When he owned up to the accounts department, he knew that he was risking his job. But the company simply told him to repay the loan in twenty-four installments.

By then, Kiran Gandhi was convinced that the inner development of people at all levels of Telco was vital to the company's success and to their own fulfillment. But how could the process be sustained in those who had attended the seminars and extended to those who had not? These concerns led him to accept a post as a training officer at the company's Management Training Center (MTC). There, he and the center's head, Nazimuddin Ahmed, set about developing an in-house training program for human development. Pandey, who saw his own experiences as "a live example of what human relations means," was also involved.

When Nazimuddin Ahmed took on the job of setting up the MTC in 1972, he thought that he had made "the biggest blunder of my life." Human development was an area that people didn't give much weight to. In planning the new training program, he says, "We were thinking about self-motivation. Really motivated people are inner-directed and not dependent on others. I said to Kiran, 'Why don't we try out the whole issue of inner change and get people to want inner change for themselves?'"

As the next step, Nazimuddin Ahmed asked some of those who had been to Asia Plateau to conduct pilot programs for a cross section of personnel in 1980. "The feedback from workers and supervisors was astonishing," he says. The issues raised ranged from small things, such as a manager's failure to offer a worker a chair, to the workers' belief that the company should house them and employ their children.

In January 1982, the MTC submitted a proposal for a series of three-day programs, conducted in Hindi, to "bring together managers, supervisors, union leaders, opinion leaders and workers to socialize in a learning atmosphere so that they may develop more open communication, greater mutual trust and a collaborative approach to solving work-related problems."[6] It was accepted, and the program was dubbed Human Relations at Work (HRW). The syllabus includes simulation and transactional analysis techniques to stimulate self-awareness, sessions on the life and values of the Tata group's founder, and conflict resolution. "It hinges on the interactions which take place between the managers, supervisors and workers who participate," comments Chandreshwar Khan.[7]

Since then, over 18,000 Telco employees have been through the course, in a plant that employs 20,000. Shop-floor workers are encouraged to lead training sessions. One observed by Michael Smith in 1993 was conducted by a worker from the toolroom, R. B. Singh. On the agenda were alcoholism, absenteeism, punctuality, synchronizing work functions, responsibility versus blame, and even blood donation schemes. In 1990, the MTC launched HRW Phase II, a refresher course for those who had already taken part in HRW I. It emphasizes the concept of listening to the inner voice, a practice that Gandhi believes lies at the core of HRW's success.

From 1983, participants were encouraged to put what they had learned at HRW into practice by setting up workplace quality circles, known as small group activities (SGAs). These bring groups of workers together for an hour each week to discuss issues of common concern. The practical results have been myriad: one group solved a fault with a metal press that had been baffling German engineers; another cut floor-cleaning time from four hours to one by building a machine out of an old lawn mower; another rigged up an exhaust fan to ease a ventilation problem that was undermining a colleague's health.

One of the first SGAs was established in the axle-part section of the works, where antagonisms among the workers were affecting quality. The SGA helped them talk through their differences, and within three months, the rejection rate of one component had fallen from 13.5 to 0.6 percent.

This SGA also addressed problems outside the factory, according to U. N. Singh, one of its leaders. One worker was so seriously in debt that his wife planned to throw herself and her children under a train. On the way to the railway track, she met one of her husband's SGA colleagues and was persuaded to turn back. "Our small group helped the family out of debt," Singh says. "One hundred fifty people contributed 20 rupees [about $1] each. A cooperative credit society helped with the rest at a much lower rate of interest." Singh maintains that the HRW courses have virtually eradicated crime in the once notorious housing colony where he lives. His family made a stand against corruption by going without electricity for thirteen years rather than paying bribes to have it installed.

HRW graduates speak of "miraculous" changes in their lives, improving their relations both at home and at work. One, a former black-marketeer, now conducts classes in values for the MTC. A case study produced by the center reports that his experiences at the HRW course and at Asia Plateau made him realize "the direction in which his children were growing due to the availability of excess money through his illegal business" and "gave him the moral strength to wriggle out of the illegal activities," in the face of threats and inducements from the mafia.[8]

Chandreshwar Khan (center) with one of Telco's problem-solving shop floor small groups

The general secretary of India's trade union congress, Shri Gopeshwar, is also the head of Telco's union. He is a firm supporter of the SGAs because they give workers a sense of belonging and a chance to express any reservations. "It's like a small family," he says. "We are going back to the old traditional way when teachers had only small groups." The groups neutralize small irritations and political provocation from outside and deal with the apprehension that workers naturally feel when faced with change.

There are also SGAs in the company's offices and hospitals. Since their founding, suggestions from the shop floor have rocketed, saving the firm millions of rupees. "Five years ago, we were quite happy with 2,500 suggestions per year, less than .25 per employee," says Sarosh Ghandy. In 1993, he expected to hit 100,000. The SGAs have helped increase productivity, and in the four-year period from 1984 to 1988, disciplinary actions against employees fell from 260 a year to 60. When intercommunal riots racked the country after the attack on the Babri mosque in Ayodhya in December 1992, the police told Ghandy that relations in the Telco area of Jamshedpur were so harmonious that they did not need to impose a curfew.

In 1986, the Asian and Pacific region of the International Confederation of Free Trade Unions (ICFTU) conducted a study on the effect of Telco's attempt to involve workers and unions. Of 153 respondents to a questionnaire on SGAs, only six thought that they had been of no benefit. "The other respondents have invariably emphasized better quality of working life, improved interpersonal relations in the work area as the benefits of small group activities, besides better work involvement and identification." Some respondents also reported improvements in their family lives and a decline in alcoholism and absenteeism. "One group reported that absenteeism, which was a high 21 percent, came down dramatically to 2.1 percent," way below the normal 10 percent.[9]

Three years later, an Indian magazine, *The Chartered Accountant*, published an article by Nazimuddin Ahmed on the effects of HRW on Telco. Among the benefits listed were a marked improvement in manager-worker relations, positive attitudes about resolving conflicts and solving problems, improved labor-management communication and cooperation, and an ability to analyze problems rather than react on a knee-jerk basis.[10]

For Sarosh Ghandy, the major benefit of HRW has been in relations between management and workers. "Our workers trust us more. They genuinely feel that we are not out to squeeze them of every last penny. And the understanding they have achieved with their managers, supervisors, and colleagues helps them to maintain the disciplined standards we require." The lack of work stoppages does not mean that there have been no disputes, but "we resolve them in a civilized manner, not by sitting on each other's heads." Ghandy believes that the firm has not sufficiently tapped the potential for grassroots leadership that the SGAs have uncovered. Full empowerment would involve slimming down the "marzipan layer" of middle management, a potential minefield.

According to Chandreshwar Khan, the courses have created "a culture of mutual trust and respect in the company. Quality of life has improved and the quality of work has improved with it. Simple phrases like 'I made a mistake,' 'You did a good job,' 'Thank you' and 'Sorry' are changing the culture of the firm."[11]

Telco's Human Relations at Work program has had numerous spin-offs in the wider community, among them the founding of Bihar's first Voluntary Blood Donors Association. Its initiator, a Bengali toolmaker at Telco, is a recovering alcoholic.

Sunil Mukherji started drinking when he was thirteen. By the time he started work at Telco, he was "drinking morning and night" and opted to work the afternoon shift because there was less supervision. He drank during his meal breaks and often failed to turn up afterwards. When his supervisor said that he would dock his pay, Mukherji threatened him with an iron rod. When drunk, he mocked and abused non-Bengalis—regardless of the offense he was causing.

The HRW sessions were "like a blow on the jaw" for Mukherji. "I felt I needed a lot of change in my life. I had betrayed my parents. I had betrayed my wife, because I came home drunk and did not care for her. I had hurt the ego of friends of other castes and races by joking about them." He wanted to make restitution for the "sugar-coated hatred of others" expressed in his jokes and hit on blood donation as a means of doing so.

In the last twelve years, Mukherji has given 300 milliliters of blood every 90 days, the legal maximum. In 1985, he set up the Voluntary Blood Donors Association of Bihar and has traveled all over the state on its behalf. Five similar associations have been established in different parts of the state, donating to 360 blood banks, forty of which are state registered.

Jamshedpur's blood bank is scrupulous about screening blood for disease. Mukherji is incensed about the laxity of other blood banks, where conditions are insanitary and patients have been given the wrong blood group.

He has a missionary zeal about blood donation as a means of breaking down communal barriers. Although, according to World Health Organization directives, patients cannot be told who donated the blood they receive, he believes that blood donation can raise awareness. "If we put Muslim blood into Hindus and vice versa, we can break down the caste system," he says. "No political organization can give integration. But blood can. How can you donate blood and then go and spill the blood of others?"

Seventy percent of his donors are villagers. Mukherji uses skits and slogans to ram the message home: "Blood is red and we are one"; "Don't shed but donate." His aim is to spread the "culture of giving blood" throughout India.

Both Tisco and Telco run rural development programs in the villages around Jamshedpur. Here too, the human development approach has had its effect.

Eleven years ago, the village of Dorkasai, some twelve miles east of Jamshedpur, was completely dependent on the monsoon for irrigation. A deep antagonism between two political leaders prevented any attempts at development. Today, Dorkasai is surrounded by 185 small ponds for irrigation and fish-farming. The income from crops and fish discourages the villagers from migrating to the cities.

The catalyst for this development was one of the two political rivals, Shailendra Kumar Mahato, an *adivasi* (aboriginal). As a young man, he dreamed of becoming a bank clerk in the city. But when he went to Jamshedpur to study, he was bullied so mercilessly by Bihari students that he left college after only six weeks. "I had thought people would want to help and cooperate with me," he remembers. "But just the opposite happened. That broke me. My ambition to succeed faded away."

He returned home with an obsessive hatred of Biharis and joined the militant Jharkhand Party, which campaigns for a separate state for the country's 30 million *adivasis*, most of whom live in Bihar. Today, he is party secretary for his district. He led protests against Bihari encroachment on *adivasi* land and campaigned for *adivasis* rather than Biharis to get the jobs in the local factory. "I led gatherings that went on violent rampages against those who settled on our land," he says. Two houses were burned down.

In need of a job, he approached Sarosh Ghandy through the leader of the Jharkhand Party and was promised a post in Telco's community services department. But the company's head of community services withdrew the offer because of Shailendra's political activities. His fury against the Biharis grew.

In 1981, Shailendra's cousin was invited to a seminar in Jamshedpur by Kiran Gandhi and Chandreshwar Khan, who hoped that it might help him with his alcohol problem. The cousin refused to go and sent Shailendra instead. Shailendra saw himself as a religious person who worshipped both as a Hindu and as an *adivasi* in the sacred village grove. He thought that the seminar, with its talk of the inner voice and personal change, had little to teach him. But he was impressed by the idea of measuring his life against moral absolutes as an objective indicator of growth. He returned home determined to make amends to his wife, the Bihari community in general, and Telco's head of community services in particular.

This was difficult enough—especially as his wife's initial response was not positive—but the real hurdle was to reconcile with his political opponent in the village, Thakurdas Mahato. He realized that their rivalry was blocking progress but could not see how to befriend a man he had always abused in the past. To his astonishment, he was welcomed with open arms. The two men began to work together.

The idea of the ponds came from S. N. Singh, the head of Telco's village development department, who had befriended Shailendra at the seminar. Shailendra started digging his first pond in June 1984, just in time to catch the monsoon rain, and stocked it with fish bought with a loan from Singh. By the end of the year, he had earned 1,300 rupees by selling fish—enough, in a country where many villagers earn no more than that in an entire year, to encourage others to follow his example. Impressed by Shailendra's enterprise, Sarosh Ghandy sanctioned the free loan of an excavator. Later, at the villagers' request, a construction company building a large canal in the area offered to help with the digging in exchange for soil to build the banks of the canal.

G. Williams

Shailendra Kumar Mahato beside one of the fishponds he introduced to his village

The moral of the story, according to S. N. Singh, is that rural development depends on people at the grassroots. "Throwing money at development is not the whole answer," he says. "We cannot do the development. The people themselves will do it around them. The development of people is crucial."

Telco's human development programs build on a tenet that might seem obvious: that people will give more to their work, and get more from it, when they feel that their input is appreciated and their welfare is considered. People who are at peace with themselves and with others have more energy to be creative.

The benefits for the company are easily measured in money saved, stoppages averted, and absenteeism reduced. The fact that Telco now produces 16,000 more trucks a year—in spite of its lack of modernization and a workforce reduction (by natural attrition) of 6,000—speaks for itself. The spin-offs for workers in terms of job satisfaction, family peace, and community development suggest that this is more than a cunning management strategy to make its "software" pay. So does the fact that the emphasis has always been on changing managers' attitudes as well as workers'.

Other Tata firms, including the Tinplate Company of India, also in Jamshedpur, have similar programs. There has been some interest from foreign companies, and Chandreshwar Khan lectures on HRW to the Confederation of Indian Industry.

The Asia Plateau seminars that served as a model for HRW won the center's founder, Rajmohan Gandhi, a gold medal for industrial peace from the Xavier Industrial Relations Institute in Jamshedpur in 1981. The citation noted that "moral regeneration [is] a necessary prerequisite for any real human and economic progress."[12]

As a writer, academic, and former member of the upper house of India's legislature, Rajmohan Gandhi has sought to express the essence of the message of his grandfather, the Mahatma, for modern India. In a recent film interview, he said:

> Take any problem you have noticed in India, whether it is the immense traffic in our towns, the immense poverty you see, the violence you read about in the newspapers. Is there some switch we can turn on which will solve these problems? I don't think so. I think millions of switches must be turned on in millions of hearts, each heart saying: my God, I'm doing so little; my God, I'm hating so much; my God, I don't care enough; I must change. We are asking every Indian to turn the searchlight inwards.[13]

In the face of vast problems, the individual approach may seem too slow, but macro solutions often collapse because it has been ignored. Telco's HRW program offers a glimpse of what the micro approach can achieve.

Notes

1. UNDP, *Human Development Report, 1994* (New York/Oxford: Oxford University Press, 1994)
2. In early 1993, my colleague Michael Smith visited Jamshedpur to research an article on Telco's Human Relations at Work program. He made his notes available to me for this chapter. Quotations come from his interviews, unless otherwise stated. See also his articles in *For a Change* (May/June 1993,

November/December 1993, February/March 1994) and in *The Financial Times* (August 25, 1993), as well as Rex Dilly's article, "Confrontation to Cooperation," in *Freeway* (December 1991). Thanks too to Kiran Gandhi for his assistance.

3. Amit Mukherjee, *The Industrial Pioneer*, December 1992.
4. R. M. Lala, *The Creation of Wealth* (Bombay: IBH Publishing Company, 1981).
5. Chandreshwar Khan, *Human Relations at Work* (unpublished paper, 1992).
6. Khan, *Human Relations at Work.*
7. Khan, *Human Relations at Work.*
8. Khan, *Human Relations at Work.*
9. ICFTU Asian and Pacific Regional Organization, *Pilot Study on Involvement of Workers and Union in Productivity and Quality Issues for the Improvement of Working Life at Telco* (1986), quoted by Kiran Gandhi in a fax to Michael Smith on March 31, 1993.
10. Nazimuddin Ahmed, "Quality Control Circle: Telco, Jamshedpur Experience," *The Chartered Accountant*, March 1989.
11. *For a Change*, October/November 1992.
12. *New World News*, March 28, 1981.
13. *Rajmohan Gandhi—Encounters with Truth* (MRA Productions, 1990).

Part III

City Lights: The North

In April 1992, Los Angeles erupted into riots. Fifty people were killed and 2,300 were injured; there was $1 billion worth of destruction.[1] The images of violence went around the world. The message was clear: something was—and is—very wrong at the core of the great cities of the industrialized world.

In 1988, 32 million Americans—and a fifth of all American children—lived below the poverty line, more than at any time since the mid-1960s.[2] Across the Atlantic in Britain, a quarter of the population lived in poverty in 1990–91 (compared with under a tenth in 1979).[3] The majority of these people live in the inner cities.

"Inner cities" is not a geographically precise definition. Southall, one of the flash points of Britain's inner-city riots in 1981, lies some ten miles west of central London, enmeshed in the metropolitan sprawl. The term covers deprived urban areas where unemployment rates are high, incomes low, services poor, and government investment meager. In the past, they were centers of manufacturing industry, drawing on the pool of local unskilled labor. Today, these industries are gone, leaving their former employees behind in a desert of joblessness.

These areas are casualties of the decline of manufacturing industry in the global North. Between 1969 and 1976, the cities of North America lost 38 million manufacturing jobs.[4] Between 1960 and 1981, British cities lost 1.7 million.[5]

Inner cities on both sides of the Atlantic are characterized by high unemployment, poverty, and crime; overstretched and underfunded social services, clinics, and schools; dilapidated housing; and degrading living conditions. In 1981–82, a researcher in the East London borough of Hackney found unemployment running at 50 percent above the national average, with 139 young people chasing every job vacancy, and a crime rate more than double the average for England and Wales. A survey of pregnant mothers in the same area in 1983 found that their average calorie intake was lower than that in Ethiopia.[6]

Little has changed in the last thirteen years. In April 1994, a British newspaper listed forty inner-city areas that "local residents, the emergency services, transport and service industry workers regard as places which, for reasons of personal safety, they would rather not visit." These areas shared "higher than average unemployment, low home ownership and a high percentage of young males with time on their hands," and many were "plagued by drugs, delinquency and violence."[7]

All over Europe, North America, Australia, and New Zealand, ethnic minorities are disproportionately affected by these trends. In 1986, in Auckland, New Zealand, three times as many Maori men were unemployed as white men.[8] In the United States, young African American men are seven times more likely to be murdered than their white counterparts.[9]

In 1993, the United Nations Development Program (UNDP) ranked the United States sixth in the world in its human development index (judged by average life expectancy, education levels, and income). But if the United States had been rated as two nations, black and white, white America would have ranked first in the world, and black America would have been thirty-first—below Barbados, Uruguay, and most members of the Organization for Economic Cooperation and Development (OECD).[10]

True, things have improved since the 1940s, when 93 percent of African Americans lived in poverty, compared with nearly a third in 1990.[11] But more than twice as many black babies still die as white ones.[12] In 1993, a quarter of all black men between the ages of twenty and sixty-four were unemployed, and a quarter of all those between sixteen and thirty were in prison.[13] These problems are most acute in the cities.

The statistics are depressing, but they are not the only reality. The inner cities of the North are places of great cultural diversity and creative energy, as demonstrated by the exuberance of London's annual Notting Hill carnival. The map of the world's great cities is sprinkled with flickering tongues of hope, where people have come together to help one another and to tackle the problems they see around them.

The next chapters focus on the struggles and achievements of six such groups, each of which draws on spiritual resources. Chapter 7 describes an initiative of one of the world's first nations, the Maori people of New Zealand, to rebuild a cultural identity eroded by colonization and migration to the cities. Chapter 8 follows the efforts of a group of ex-offenders to provide resources for an inner-city community in London. Chapter 9 visits the northern English city of Bradford, where people of different faiths are working to build bridges across the cultural divide. Chapter 10 tells the story of a group of African American teenagers who have been making a bid to outlaw violence in the schools of Atlanta, Georgia. Chapter 11 describes the work of community development veteran John Perkins. And Chapter 12 looks at an innovative attempt by a church in Pasadena, California, to build coalitions to meet the needs of the city's young people.

Notes

1. *U.S. News & World Report,* May 31, 1993.
2. Alan B. Durning, "Ending Poverty," in *State of the World, 1990: Worldwatch Institute Report* (New York: W. W. Norton, 1990).
3. *The Independent,* September 1, 1993.
4. Herbert Girardet, *The Gaia Atlas of Cities* (London: Gaia Books, 1992).
5. Colin Ward, *Welcome, Thinner City* (London: Bedford Square Press, 1989).
6. Paul Harrison, *Inside the Inner City* (London: Penguin Books, 1992).
7. *The Independent on Sunday,* April 17, 1994.
8. Ranginui Walker, *Ka Whawhai Tonu Matou: Struggle Without End* (Auckland: Penguin Books, 1990).

9. *The Independent,* December 14, 1993.

10. UNDP, *Human Development Report, 1993* (New York/Oxford: Oxford University Press, 1993).

11. *The Oregonian,* August 9, 1992.

12. UNDP, *Human Development Report, 1993.*

13. *U.S. News & World Report,* May 31, 1993.

CHAPTER 7

Standing Tall
in New Zealand

Maori people had been living on the islands of New Zealand for centuries before they were "discovered" by Dutch explorer Abel Tasman in 1640. They had developed a rich culture in which respect for the community and the environment was based on a deep spiritual awareness. For them, as for most of the world's indigenous peoples, the encounter with Europeans was disastrous. It decimated their numbers and robbed them of their land, culture, language, and identity.

For decades, Maori people have been hugely overrepresented in New Zealand's dole queues and prisons and underrepresented in higher education and white-collar jobs. But today they are winning back their pride and identity, thanks to a reassertion of Maori culture and values nurtured in hundreds of preschool *kohanga reo* (language nests) across the country.

Kohanga Reo has been described as "the most significant thing that happened to the Maori people this century."[1] Dr. Tamati Reedy, former secretary of the Department of Maori Affairs, maintains, "Kohanga Reo is providing the fundamental shift that is going on in the minds of our people, that we can lift ourselves up, we don't have to depend on anyone else."[2] The impact on the groups of Maori adults who run the *kohanga* is as significant as the effect on the 14,000 preschool children who attend them.

Traditional Maori society focused on the extended family (*whanau*), the subtribe (*hapu*), and the tribe (*iwi*).[3] The *whanau* spanned the generations from the elders (*kaumatua*) to the grand-children (*mokopuna*) and great-grandchildren; it might include twenty to thirty people sharing one or more sleeping houses. Responsibility was collective and communal: for instance, all adults stood in loco parentis to the children, and land belonged not to individuals but to subtribes. The heart of the commu-nity was the *marae*, the sacred tribal meeting place.

For Maori, all living things and even places have a life force (*mauri*), as do human beings. The land is seen as the mother of all living things. From this, Maori derive a genealogy (*whaka-papa*) that gives them respect for the environment, explains Donna Awatere-Huata, a Maori businesswoman and activist. "It's taught us caution—we've learnt to live in harmony with the shrub, with the fly and all other living creatures," she told the World Indigenous Peoples Conference in Ngaruawahia in 1990. "*Whakapapa* makes us rooted: 'I'm related to that fern, so I'll think twice before I boot it into the water.'"

The Europeans left New Zealand in peace for over a century after Tasman's voyage. Then, in 1769, James Cook explored its coasts and found large colonies of seals and stands of trees. By the end of the century, European sealers and traders had followed in his wake. At the time of Cook's voyage, there are thought to have been at least 200,000 Maori people in New Zealand.[4] By 1840, European diseases and tribal wars using European mus-kets had cut this population by two-fifths. Fifty years later, according to the census of 1892, the Maori numbered only 42,000.

In 1840, in response to requests from both Maori elders and European settlers for some form of regulation, the British Crown signed the Treaty of Waitangi with over 500 Maori chiefs. The Maori signatories believed that they were handing over not the "substance" of their land but its "shadow"; they were under the impression that ultimate sovereignty still rested in their hands. The English believed that sovereignty had been ceded. This con-fusion was assisted by the fact that the Maori translation of the text did not tally with the English original.[5]

The treaty gave the Crown the sole right to buy land, but only when Maori wanted to sell. As settlers poured into New

Zealand during the second half of the century, the authorities found more and more ways to persuade or force Maori communities to part with their property. By the early twentieth century, Europeans had bought—or confiscated, in what historian Keith Sinclair describes as the "worst injustice ever perpetrated by a New Zealand government"[6]—most of New Zealand's North Island. Much of what was left in Maori hands was either leased to Europeans or economically worthless. For a people whose identity and status were tightly bound up with communal land-ownership, the loss was profound.

After the census of 1896, the Maori population began to rise again, partly because of an increasing resistance to European diseases. But the government policy of assimilation continued to eat away at cultural pride and identity. This process accelerated after World War II, as Maori people moved into the cities and traditional tribal and family ties weakened. In 1930, 90 percent of Maori lived in the country;[7] by 1976, 76 percent lived in the towns.[8]

"Assimilation meant in practice the imposition of the dominant Pakeha [white] culture in the public sphere of life in New Zealand," stated a government report in 1988. "Minority group members were forced to limit the use of their own cultural ways to their homes or other private domains of society such as voluntary associations." But, it added, the policy was not successful: Maori culture continued to play a major role in the lives of Maori people.[9]

In spite of this resilience, schools committed to assimilating Maori children into white society nearly killed off the Maori language. From 1847, all teaching was in English. From 1905, children were discouraged from speaking Maori on school premises. Donna Awatere-Huata remembers how this affected her father and his contemporaries:

> They didn't want us to hear them reciting *whakapaka* for fear we would become tainted by the language. They believed the idea that we had to have English and a Western education if we were to succeed. We can only imagine the kind of deep hurt that they must have gone through as young children going to school and being hit, some

of them, for speaking Maori, and their anxiety was to do anything to help their children avoid that kind of pain. It has led to several generations who cannot speak the language.[10]

In 1900, 90 percent of all Maori children entering primary school spoke Maori as their first language; by 1960, only 26 percent did so.[11] A survey between 1973 and 1978 found only one community in the country where Maori was a living language used between parents and children. The number of children who spoke Maori as their first language could be "counted on the fingers of one hand," says Dr. Richard Benton, who conducted the survey for the New Zealand Council for Educational Research.[12]

With the language went culture and confidence. Maori children did poorly in school: in 1965, over 85 percent left secondary school without qualifications. During the next two decades, Maori language and culture were introduced into school curricula, but 75 percent of Maori teenagers still failed to achieve any qualifications.

The 1986 census for Auckland city found under a fifth of Maori in tertiary education, compared with nearly two-fifths of Pakehas; a third of Maori in white-collar jobs, against two-thirds of whites; and 12.1 percent of Maori men and 15.9 percent of Maori women unemployed, against 4.7 and 7.3 percent of white men and women, respectively. Of New Zealand's 404,185 Maori people, 2.7 percent were in prison, compared with 0.2 percent of the rest of the population.[13]

By the mid-1970s, it was clear to Maori professionals that the government's top-down approach to the "Maori problem" was not working. Something had to be done. It began with a radical shift of policy at the Department of Maori Affairs.

One of those at the heart of these changes was Iritana Tawhi-whirangi, now general manager of the National Kohanga Reo Trust Board. She grew up in Ngati Porou, a tribal area much influenced by Maori politician and elder statesman Sir Apirana Ngata. He was a firm believer in drawing the best from both

Western and Maori education. In 1949, he wrote in a child's autograph book:

> Grow up tender plant in the dawn of your world.
> Turn your hands to the tools of the Pakeha for the well-being of your body.
> Turn your heart to the treasures of your ancestors as a plume for your brow.
> Give your soul unto God the author of all things.

Following his advice, the elders "went after the tools," says Tawhiwhirangi, and sent their young people away to white schools. "But they didn't keep our cultural cloak around us," she says. Her generation, born in the late 1920s and early 1930s, did not miss out as seriously as later ones, however. "We still grew up at the feet of our elders, in that culture, confident about our identity. The next generation didn't have that cultural support we had."[14] By the end of his life, Ngata believed that the quest for Pakeha education had gone too far and wrote of "thousands of Maori old and young who entered the schools of this country and poured out, with their minds closed to the culture which is their inheritance."[15]

Mrs. Tawhiwhirangi went into teaching and describes a turning point when, after working with older pupils, she became a teacher of infants. "In working with those forty-eight children, the first thing I realized was that there was no way that I could do justice to each of them. So I rounded up the parents and said, 'I need you to come in.'" When the parents protested that they were not teachers, she told them that their role was to talk to and affirm the children. "Within weeks they became involved in the classroom dynamic. Seeing how the latent talent of those people surfaced was just magic."[16] The idea of parental involvement was to be central to Kohanga Reo.

Later, at the urging of her tribal elders, she worked as a welfare officer for the Department of Maori Affairs, which was much criticized at the time for fostering dependency. What she found, both in rural Ruatoria and in the city of Wellington, did little to shake that assessment. People seemed to expect the professionals to do everything for them; some dropped off application forms for her to fill in that they could have completed themselves. "You do need these professional people, but what Maoridom was doing was leaving it to them. That was a reflection of the way society had bred people. You breed those that can, those that can't."[17]

She was shattered by the low self-worth of the Maori people in the city. "Back home, you might have been poor, but you were proud in your poverty, you learnt to share what you had." Her colleagues were startled when she spent office time visiting Maori families and getting to know them. "What Maori people were crying out for was for Maori people who could identify with them—not people who wanted them to be more like white people. Until you can make people feel that they have value, until you can give people dignity, until you can let them believe that there is a place for them under the sun, they're not going to pass happy vibes to their children."

A group of senior Maori welfare officers began to get together to discuss these issues. "We concluded that there are two sides: a positive and a negative side. The focus had been too much on the negative. We said that nobody was to speak of a Maori problem again. We know the problems absolutely, but we keep wallowing in them. This time we're going to leave them aside and talk about the joy, the wonder, the beauty of being Maori." They asked the minister of Maori affairs, Duncan McIntyre, for a government review of Maori perceptions of the department. It was undertaken by Kara Puketapu, a Maori public servant, who was then appointed secretary of the Maori Affairs Department to implement the neccessary changes.

Within a week of his appointment, Puketapu called Mrs. Tawhiwhirangi and six other Maori welfare officers to his office and gave them twenty-four hours in which to redesign the department's policies in response to the review. "What do we do but pick up a pen and start to write?" remembers Tawhiwhirangi. "For twenty-four hours we never even had time to talk together or to proofread our work."[18] Puketapu was

E. Peters

Iritana Tawhiwhirangi: "the joy of being Maori"

disgusted with their efforts: "What you have proposed, all other departments are doing also, probably better than this one." He gave them another twenty-four hours. "This time," he said, "think Maori."

"From that point on," says Iritana Tawhiwhirangi, "we never spoke English; we spoke Maori. We realized that our practice of orally debating important issues in the *marae* forum was what we should be doing. And, having returned to that practice, within half a day the policy of Tu Tangata [stand tall] was born."[19]

Tu Tangata sparked off a whole range of programs, including youth and women's workshops, skills centers, a job-search program for the unemployed, and a fostering program that returned young Maori to the care of their tribal groups. Each program was created in response to concerns expressed at tribal *hui* (meetings) and endorsed by the tribe. The emphasis was on empowerment and self-help and on a Maori modus operandi based on collective decision making and responsibility. The "jewel in the crown" of these programs, in the words of historian Ranginui Walker, was Kohanga Reo.

In 1980, a large tribal *hui* agreed that Maoridom must take action to preserve the Maori language. The seed thought for Kohanga Reo came from an elder who said, "When a child is born, take it, put it to the breast, and begin speaking Maori at that point." The idea was to set up preschools, run by the community, where children would be totally immersed in Maori language and culture. In the process, the adults involved would also develop. The model would be the *whanau*, spanning the generations from grandparents to grandchildren, even though those involved might not be related to one another.

The first *kohanga* opened in Pukeatua in 1982 and was quickly followed by four other pilot schemes. The idea took off like wildfire. Within a year, there were 107. By the end of 1985, there were 377 *kohanga*, and fifty-four district training branches had been set up. Three years later, over 500 *kohanga* catered to some 8,000 children, about 15 percent of Maori children under age five.[20] Nearly half of these *kohanga* were sited on *marae*, with others in community centers, schools, homes, and churches. The umbrella organization, the Te Kohanga Reo National Trust, set itself the target of reaching 75 percent of Maori children by 1998. By 1994, some 14,000 children were enrolled.

In the early days, each *kohanga* was given seed funding of NZ$5,000 (US$3,200) in its first year, with a warning that, on average, another NZ$45,000 would have to be raised. After that, it received an operating grant of NZ$18,000 a year. The shortfall in running costs was made up by contributions from parents, sometimes in the form of a set fee, and by fund-raising activities. In the first three years, the government contributed NZ$1.5 million, and the *whanau* raised about NZ$30 million.

E. Peters

Traditional Maori teaching in a pre-school language nest (kohanga reo)

A government review in 1988 reckoned that the *whanau*-government funding ratio stood at roughly 60:40.²¹

These funding arrangements made for self-sufficiency and independence but placed a heavy burden on the mostly female *whanau*: Maori women are New Zealand's poorest group. The review team in 1988 found that many *whanau* believed that the government should be giving the same support to *kohanga* as it gave to state preschoools—not just for financial reasons, but because they saw such funding as a public statement about the movement's standing. In 1990, the *kohanga* were placed on the same financial footing as other preschools, with a full government grant on a per-child basis.

The ethos of the *kohanga reo* is holistic, and the educational style is traditional, using storytelling, dance, drama, games, ritual, prayer, and meditation. A retired Pakeha headmistress writes of a visit to three *kohanga* in 1994: "The learning experiences witnessed were quite enthralling. Delightful young three- to five-year-olds, healthy, clean, highly motivated, eagerly entering into the prayer, worship and language-learning as well as reading experience. Having taught Maori students in a minority situation in many schools, I could feel the difference which was being achieved."[22]

The *whanau* embraces a wide age range, from the fluent speakers (*kaiako*)—mostly of grandparent age—through parents and young people down to the children themselves. In 1988, some 4,000 adults were involved in *kohanga*—2,000 of them elders. Ninety percent of them were unpaid volunteers.

The aim of the *kohanga* goes beyond the children to the revitalization of the community as a whole. Because all members of the *whanau* are involved in every aspect of running the *kohanga*—and all learning is undertaken collectively—those involved acquire a wide range of skills. Not only the children but also the adults reestablish contact with their language and culture. For many, this is a transforming experience. At a recent *hui*, a *kohanga* organizer described how she used to while away her days at the bingo hall, until someone began to talk up the idea of opening a local *kohanga*. Eventually, five parents were convinced, and the *kohanga* opened in 1983. She is now at the *kohanga* at 7:30 every morning to receive the early arrivals, has learned to speak Maori, and, according to an observer, "her motivation, energy and commitment are rocketing."[23]

With fluent speakers in short supply, some *kohanga* are more effective than others. But even the weakest go some way toward rebuilding the communal links that were shattered when Maori people moved to the cities. "Even in small struggling *kohanga* where there may be almost no Maori spoken, no adults with the language and few *whanau* links beyond the children's parents, the *kaupapa* [ethos] has a symbolic value," concluded the government review of 1988. "Families, who could otherwise be isolated, support each other in a common endeavor, and through this, feel linked to the wider network of Maori development."

The spin-offs have been impressive. In 1984, there were about 150 Maori women in business; in 1990, there were over 5,000. "When we interviewed some of those women, nearly all of them had a *kohanga* management experience," says Donna Awatere-Huata. "Kohanga is doing it for us women. We're recapturing all those stunning management skills that our ancestors were just brilliant at, that we practice whenever we have a *hui*."[24] A review of small businesses found that only 15 to 20 percent of those run by Maori collapsed within the first two years, compared with 70 to 75 percent of those run by Pakeha.

"The ultimate objective of Te Kohanga Reo is nothing less than the rebirth of the Maori nation as an equal but separate element contributing to the common good of New Zealand society," stated Koro Wetere, minister of Maori affairs in 1987.[25]

In spite of the successes of Kohanga Reo, the battle for the Maori language is not over. Fluent speakers are dying faster than new ones are being taught. And there are concerns about what happens to *kohanga* graduates when they move on to primary school. The government review found that many children lost the Maori language within one term of moving up: the experience of being a minority in an alien environment undermined their enthusiasm for being Maori.

The tribal meetings consulted by the review team in 1988 expressed a sense of urgency about these difficulties. "They could not afford the luxury of developing slowly over many years as had the kindergarten, playcenter and child care movements. The preservation of the language and culture, the strengthening of the *whanau* and the empowering of the people required widespread, effective action now."[26] Dr. Richard Benton echoes their concern: "The statistics are still against us. There's no room for complacency. Pressure groups are very important. We need unremitting effort."[27]

One response has been to encourage state primary schools to set up bilingual units and to become more sensitive to Maori culture. Other groups of parents have gone outside the system altogether and set up their own Maori primary schools. The aim is not separatism but biculturalism. Peter Sharples, one of the prime movers in the Maori schools initiatives, sees it as "providing Maori options." A monocultural educational system has produced a system in which Maori "have to fit in and be Maori part time." The new schools will produce "kids who value things

Maori and are able to include it in their lifestyle and their vocation. They will bring status to things Maori and insist that things are done in a Maori fashion as well as a European fashion. What you'll get is a more meaningful Maori input into New Zealand society."[28]

Kohanga Reo is unique among the examples in this book in being a government program. It is typical, however, in that it depends on grassroots initiative and empowerment and draws on spiritual resources. It offers the hope of a rebirth of dignity and pride not just for Maori people themselves but for first nations everywhere—and for the immigrants who have come to their lands and have much to learn from the original inhabitants.

Ultimately, Iritana Tawhiwhitangi hopes that Kohanga Reo will be coordinated not by a central national trust but by the *iwi* (tribes). She looks back at the birth of the *tu tangata* policy and says, "Kohanga Reo was when we were able to dot the *i*'s, cross the *t*'s, and move thousands of people in a way that in all my life I have never seen before. I have nothing but the greatest admiration for Maori people who, ten years ago, said: 'We can't do it,' and who today are telling us how it should be done."[29]

Notes

1. Interview with Peter Sharples by Edward and Elisabeth Peters in March 1991 for an article on Kohanga Reo in *For a Change*, May 1991. I am grateful to them for making the texts of their interviews available to me for this chapter, and to Joan Holland for her assistance in gathering other material.
2. Interview with Dr. Tamati Reedy by Edward and Elisabeth Peters, December 1990.
3. Ranginui Walker, *Ka Whawhai Tonu Matou: Struggle Without End* (Auckland: Penguin Books, 1990).
4. Keith Sinclair, *A History of New Zealand* (Auckland: Penguin Books, 1988).
5. Walker, *Ka Whawhai Tonu Matou*.
6. Sinclair, *History of New Zealand*, 143.
7. Walker, *Ka Whawhai Tonu Matou*.
8. Sinclair, *History of New Zealand*.
9. *Government Review of Te Kohanga Reo*, 1988.

10. Donna Awatere-Huata, speech to the World Indigenous Peoples Conference, Ngaruawahia, December 1990.
11. Walker, *Ka Whawhai Tonu Matou.*
12. Interview with Dr. Richard Benton by Edward and Elisabeth Peters, March 1991.
13. Walker, *Ka Whawhai Tonu Matou.*
14. Judith Manchester and Anne O'Rourke, *Liberating Learning: Women as Facilitators of Learning* (Aotearoa: Whakatu Wahini, 1993), 177.
15. Walker, *Ka Whawhai Tonu Matou,* 193.
16. Manchester and O'Rourke, *Liberating Learning,* 179.
17. Conversation between Iritana Tawhiwhirangi and Edward and Elisabeth Peters, December 1990. All unreferenced quotations from Mrs. Tawhiwhirangi are from this source.
18. Manchester and O'Rourke, *Liberating Learning,* 180.
19. Manchester and O'Rourke, *Liberating Learning,* 180–81.
20. *Government Review of Te Kohanga Reo.*
21. *Government Review of Te Kohanga Reo.*
22. Letter from Joan Holland, May 1994.
23. Holland letter.
24. Awatere-Huata, speech to World Indigenous Peoples Conference.
25. *Government Review of Te Kohanga Reo.*
26. *Government Review of Te Kohanga Reo.*
27. Benton interview.
28. Sharples interview.
29. Manchester and O'Rourke, *Liberating Learning,* 181.

CHAPTER 8

London: New Life
in the Inner City

On April 17, 1994, *The Independent on Sunday* printed a list of forty "no-go" areas in Britain's inner cities. Among them was the Stonebridge Estate, a public-housing development in the London borough of Brent. Since 1981, it has been the home of what has been called "the most ambitious grassroots-led community group in Britain."[1]

Brent has the highest concentration of black people of any borough in Britain. In 1981, a third of its population was black, with the proportion in Stonebridge and neighboring developments ranging from nearly two-fifths to over half. One in ten people in Brent was unemployed, and one in six in Stonebridge. Two-fifths of all families in Stonebridge were headed by a single parent, compared with one-fifth in the borough as a whole.[2]

Over the past thirteen years, Stonebridge has been the site of a brave attempt by a group of young ex-offenders to help their community break out of the cycle of poverty, powerlessness, and crime. Their flagship has been Bridge Park, the largest black-run community center in Europe. Its history has been checkered. Opened with much fanfare by Prince Charles in 1988, it ran into serious financial difficulties and, as I write, is in the hands of the official receiver. The story of its creators illustrates both the vitality and the problems of spiritually driven grassroots initiatives.

The founders of the Harlesden People's Community Council (HPCC) are first-generation black British.[3] Their parents,

112

recent immigrants from the Caribbean, had struggles of their own: being transplanted into a new culture, cut off from close family ties, and having to cope with racism at work. Of the five men most closely involved with the HPCC in recent years, only one, Mike Wilson, stayed in school and went to college. The others describe themselves as "graduates of the academy of the streets."

Leonard Johnson, Lawrence Fearon, Delaney Brown, and Errol Williams grew up close to one another in Harlesden (an area of Brent that includes Stonebridge), running with gangs and getting into trouble with the police. Peer pressures were strong and incentives to go straight weak. Williams, who learned bricklaying in Borstal (a youth custody facility), describes starting work on a building site: "A friend I used to get into trouble with came by and asked what I was doing. He went into his pocket and pulled out a lot of money and said, 'This is what I just earned.' I walked straight off the site."

As young men, they each came to a turning point that led them away from crime into community action. All four are now evangelical Christians and say that it is their faith that inspired and sustained them.

Delaney Brown's parents sent him to Sunday school, but he started stealing when he was fourteen. It was a form of business: he knew what people wanted, where to steal it, and where to sell it. "Ninety percent of my life was crime," he says. At the same time, he knew that he would one day become a Christian, "but in my time."

When he was eighteen, he and two friends were arrested for picking pockets. Although on this occasion they were innocent, they were found guilty. Brown was sentenced to three months at a detention center. Right after his hearing, the doctor ruled him unfit to serve his sentence on the grounds of a leg injury (sustained during a burglary six months earlier). He was sent back to the magistrates, who, to his astonishment, released him on bail. Waiting outside the court for his friends to be driven away, he had a "dialogue with God": "OK God, I understand that you don't want me to go to prison for stealing. OK, no more stealing."

He stopped stealing but went on selling dope. Two years later, he decided to stop that too when he saw some girls smoking cocaine in a club and realized that they were bringing up the next generation. It hit him that if things went on this way, in a generation's time, "we would still be at the bottom of the pile as black people."

Meanwhile, Brown's closest friends, Johnson and Fearon, had been in Borstal and prison. Johnson had been thrown out of school at the age of fifteen, ran his own gang, and ended up serving a four-year sentence for burglary. In prison, he began reading books by Martin Luther King, Malcolm X, and Stokely Carmichael and was intrigued by how often the Bible was quoted. He went to the source and was hooked. "The Bible was like a magnet," he says. "It began to convert me." Eventually, he broke down, alone in his cell, and told God, "If you can change me, I'll spend the rest of my life helping other people, to pay back for what I've done."

Johnson started to avoid some of his friends and stopped smoking and getting visitors to bring him "illegal" items. "I felt I had to do these things to let God come into my life," he says. To his surprise, he was granted parole after only nineteen months, in spite of the fact that he had another case outstanding against him.

Adapting to life outside was tough. Johnson was embarassed by his conversion and tried to keep it quiet, but his friends noticed a change. "Most of them didn't accept it," he says. "Some stopped talking to me. My car tires were getting slashed, my life was being threatened. I was told to leave the street."

One night he ran into Lawrence Fearon at a party. Fearon had also just left prison, determined to go straight. Two things had made him reconsider his life: a fire at his apartment, in which he and his girlfriend lost all their possessions, and a stretch in Ford open prison, where he met long-term prisoners whose families had grown up while they were inside. "I realized that this wasn't where I wanted my life to lead," he says. Back on the streets, Fearon felt uncomfortable with his old lifestyle: "I was beginning to wonder if there was something wrong with me."

The two men talked about their dilemma. Johnson compared it to being caught in a whirlpool, jumping from one boat to another: parties, fighting, women, clothes, crime. "The whirlpool was dragging us under and we weren't noticing it. I told Lawrence that I had jumped out and was swimming to the shore." They left the party and began to talk about what they could do for their community.

Their first attempts were erratic. Johnson went out on the streets at night, looking for muggers and trying to talk them out of it. He'd march into pubs, bang the table for silence, and harangue the drinkers and gamblers: "I was trying to tell them we could do better with our lives." They called meetings, and eventually large numbers began to turn up to talk about what was needed in the community. One of the prime movers at this stage was Juliet Simpson, a young woman who lived in the Stonebridge Estate.

In the spring of 1981, Johnson, Fearon, and Simpson, along with four other friends, set up the Harlesden People's Community Council (HPCC). They took over the Annexe, an underused youth club, and started running drama, dancing, and other classes; a Sunday school; and mother and toddler groups. To give the young people an alternative to petty crime, Johnson got hold of cheap watches and clothes for them to sell. Fearon called him a "legitimate hustler." With the money they raised, they gave out small loans. They began to build a relationship with the police, which meant that they could liaise with them when people got arrested and confront them on issues of police harassment.

The atmosphere in Stonebridge was highly charged. In April 1981, there were riots in Brixton, in south London. In July, a wave of rioting engulfed twenty-two inner-city areas, with the worst outbreaks in Liverpool and Manchester and in Southall and Brixton in London. Johnson went around Stonebridge telling people, "We're not going to riot here." One Friday night, things came to a head. Youths gathered outside the Annexe, where there was a disco, and the police lined up with riot shields. Johnson and Simpson came out of the Annexe and shouted to the crowds, urging them not to destroy everything they had just begun to build in the community. "If you're determined to riot, go and do it somewhere else. This area is depressed enough already." People began to drop their weapons and drift away.

The riots focused national and local concern on the inner cities. The HPCC's role in averting a riot in Stonebridge brought them to the attention of the local government, the Brent Council, which arranged for its policy coordinator, Richard Gutch, to help the HPCC articulate what should be done. One of their recommendations was the creation of a major facility for the community. When a local bus depot came onto the market, Johnson and Fearon saw its potential. At a meeting in September, the owners of the depot agreed to give the HPCC six months to raise the £1.8 million (US$2.8 million) to buy it. At a noisy session packed with members of the community, the council agreed to help find the money. Gutch and the HPCC set to work on a feasibility study.

Delaney Brown was skeptical when he first discovered what was going on. "I was trying to rebuild my life," he says. "When Leonard and Lawrence talked about getting grants from the council, my impression was that they were going to rip the council off, so I wasn't interested. It was only when I discovered that they were reading the Bible that I knew they'd changed. They used to be blasphemous to the point that I'd walk away because I thought lightning was going to strike them."

Errol Williams also started to work with the HPCC toward the end of 1981. He and his gambling friends in the pubs used to call Johnson the "mad preacher." What changed his mind was the prospect of working in an office. "At school I'd always wanted to be my own boss, have a desk and chair and telephone and put my feet up." He took over running the HPCC classes, living off his unemployment benefit and $19 expenses a week— a big drop from the $300 or more he could make gambling. He says that he had become fed up with the cheating—and the physical danger if one got caught—and was looking for a way to give it up. The HPCC provided the alternative he needed.

P. Carr

Leonard Johnson: "trying to tell them we could do better with our lives"

Johnson, a natural leader and visionary, was convinced the £1.8 million would come through. Fearon had his doubts. At midnight that Christmas Eve, he stopped on his way home through a park near the bus depot and prayed for a sign. "I felt a warmth come over me," he remembers. "I felt very calm, as if God was present. When I looked up, I could see the bus garage in the distance, and it was all lit up. There were people moving about in it and it was like the place was already up and running. I knew the thing was going to work."

After six months of negotiation, and just ahead of deadline, grants came in from the national, metropolitan, and local governments to meet the bill. Mike Wilson, who took part in the early meetings with the Brent Council, sees the council's decision to back the project as good economics. "You either spend £20 million [US$30 million], which is what the Brixton riots cost in terms of the damage done, or you invest in the community." In February 1994, with the bailiffs at the door, he still reckoned that Brent had gotten a bargain. "They've spent or mobilized about £13 million [US$20 million] over a number of years instead of what they could have spent in one," he said. The creation of Bridge Park, with facilities requested by the community, eased the frustration that could have erupted in further trouble.

The HPCC moved into its new offices on May 5, 1982, and set about raising the money for the center. A local firm gave them old office furniture, which they renovated and sold. "We were very strong on doing things for ourselves and very critical of others," says Fearon. But the sums required were so great that they found themselves depending more and more on grants.

Grants came from the European Social Fund, the Department of the Environment, the Urban Programme, and the Brent Council. They used the European money to raise the wages of people employed through the Manpower Services Commission, a government training scheme attacked by the Left as "slave labor." In the years up to 1988, over 400 people were trained through this and other schemes while working on the site. Among them were the HPCC members themselves; they understudied professionals who were employed to teach themselves out of their jobs. HPCC also set up its own building company to do some of the building work.

The first phase of the scheme—including the Information Technology Center (ITEC) and a preschool center—was completed by March 1983. The ITEC went on to become the Middlesex ITEC, which now trains over 250 people a year. The second phase was dogged by conflicts with unsatisfactory architects, control struggles with the council, and troubles with some of the professional staff. In July 1985, the project's finance manager and his assistant made off with £50,000 from the project's bank account. As the years dragged on and the HPCC got more tied up in red tape, the community itself got impatient, and some of the founders, including Juliet Simpson, moved on.

Finally, in October 1987, the complex was completed. It boasted a 1,250-seat gymnasium, squash courts, a sauna, and physiotherapy rooms; thirty-two units for starter businesses; training and seminar rooms; a recording studio; and a bar, restaurant, and hall for 400 people. Bridge Park was becoming famous as a symbol of inner-city hope: its founders were invited to meet the Royal Family; they attended conferences overseas and were taken up by the Conservative government. Celebrities flocked to see Bridge Park. On December 20, 1988, the center was officially opened by Prince Charles.

Interviewed on television that year, Leonard Johnson summed up what Bridge Park meant for Stonebridge: "It's a way of showing people on the streets, people without academic qualifications, people who don't think they are able to make headway in life, that they have skills to offer, that they are not written off, that determination and belief can also carry them forward."

In 1989, its first year of full operation, Bridge Park earned 52 percent of its total income, and Brent Council promised an annual grant of £365,000 (US$569,000) for the next five years. A consultants' report urged expansion, with the inclusion of private-sector representatives on the board. Three years later, at the end of March 1992, the council withdrew its funding. Since then, the center has been run by volunteers and has lived off its rents. By February 1994, it had debts of £1 million (US$1.5 million) and was being taken to court by Brent. What went wrong?

Both sides agree that the skills needed to manage a multi-million-dollar building are different from those required to get it off the ground, though opinions differ as to whether the HPCC could have swung it with more support and training. It's clear, too, that Britain's dive into recession in the late 1980s came at just the wrong time for Bridge Park. As the recession deepened, the private sector had less money to spend, and the central government stepped up pressure on local governments to cut back on services. "Bridge Park came to us for money three times a year for four years," says Charles Wood, the chief executive of Brent (a nonpolitical post). "The council began to feel that at a time when we were having to close down old people's homes and schools in an already deprived area, it was difficult to be putting half a million pounds into a hole."

There was a political factor too. The project had been launched with the help of a Labour council, which believed in subsidy, at a time when the Conservative national government was trying to force local governments to economize. Initially, according to

Richard Gutch, the HPCC tended more toward the Conservative rhetoric of "individual entrepreneurship, getting up and doing for themselves rather than relying on the welfare state." The HPCC thought that it would not need public money once Bridge Park was up and running. This made the HPCC popular with the national government but was unrealistic.

In 1991, control of the council passed into the hands of the Conservatives, who urged commercial viability. By then, the HPCC knew that Bridge Park could not break even on its own and depended on council grants. "If we set commercial prices, then the community couldn't afford to use Bridge Park, even though it was built for them," says Errol Williams, who took over from Johnson as chairman in 1992. "If we charged community rates, we wouldn't be able to make funds to run Bridge Park."

The trigger for Brent's withdrawal was a critical report by its auditors, which revealed the extent of Bridge Park's debts and suggested financial irregularities. The audit was forwarded to the Fraud Squad, amidst adverse publicity, but has not led to any action. "I'm not going to say no stealing has gone on in Bridge Park," says Williams. "But my conscience bears me witness that there's been no fraudulent dealings by its founders or the board. Do you think if Brent could have found any fraud we would still be here?" Gutch, who worked closely with the HPCC until he left Brent town hall in 1985, is inclined to agree. But he thinks that some employees may have exploited a lax regime.

Gutch attributes many of Bridge Park's problems to a lack of people with the professional expertise to handle the bureaucratic and management side. Of the core group, only Mike Wilson started out with the report-writing and budget-making skills required for a large-scale project. From the outset, town hall officials expressed concern about handing public money over to inexperienced people—particularly ones with criminal records. Some would have been happier if the project had been under direct council control, though Gutch is convinced that this would not have worked.

The danger in such circumstances, he says, is that outsiders try to take over. "The issue is how to help in a way that is enabling and empowering." This is no academic question for Gutch. He recalls an early disastrous attempt to draft a document *for* the HPCC rather than working it through *with* the members. "They were really critical that they hadn't been involved. We started again. I talked with them about each chapter, wrote it up, gave them each a copy, revised it—and in the end we had a document that they felt reflected what they wanted. It was very labor-intensive. After I left, I don't think there was anyone who tried to perform that role—keeping a watchful eye, advising, helping the group to take more responsibility and control." Without someone to interpret them to each other, relations between the council and the HPCC spun into a downward spiral.

Maurice Forsyth, principal field officer for Britain's Commission for Racial Equality, sees this as a classic case of an imaginative program whose initiators were not given enough support. Mike Wilson, general manager from 1985 to 1990 and now acting company secretary, agrees. "There tends to be a lot of underinvestment in people who are working in front-line situations, where, if nothing is done, people will suffer," he says. The HPCC was torn in two trying to run the development and placate the officials on the one hand and trying to keep the community happy on the other.

The divorce between Brent and Bridge Park has been bitter, with accusations of dishonesty and incompetence from one side, and of racism and ingratitude from the other. "We're being told we're good enough to have initiated this, to have brought Prince Charles here, to have attracted millions of pounds, to have stopped two riots, but we are not good enough to stay and run it," says Williams.

For the HPCC, the issue of whether Bridge Park remains in black hands has been vital. "We don't want it to be, 'We gave them the money and they screwed up. Blacks are incompetent,'" explained Brown early in 1994. The creation of the center gave a tremendous boost to the black community; the discouraging effect of its loss would be just as great, he believed.

The core group at the heart of the HPCC shares a strong evangelical Christian faith. For Johnson, Fearon, Brown, and Wilson, it is what brought them into community work in the first place; for Williams, it developed in the process. Fearon maintains that only a spiritual encounter could have liberated him from his sense of inferiority and given him the courage to embark on the bus garage project. "It was incredibly ambitious," says Richard Gutch. "They needed something to make them believe it was all going to happen—either religious faith or a pretty strong commitment to the idea. They had both."

Every morning since 1984, the members of the HPCC have met to study the Bible and pray together. "If we hadn't had that spiritual fellowship, our relationships would have gone out the window," says Fearon. They pray for the council as well as for themselves. "We have faced every situation with prayer and determination, and in every situation so far we've found a solution," says Mike Wilson. Their catchprase is, "God, we can't wait to see how you're going to get us out of this one!"

The downside of this faith in God's provision, according to Gutch, has been a tendency toward overoptimism, particularly in the early days. There was a feeling that God was with them and that it would always be that way. The convictions of the inner core may also have alienated people of different views who wanted to work with the HPCC. They certainly contributed to the reservations of some at town hall. "They were passing over public money in the form of Urban Aid Grants," explains Gutch. "Usually that can't be given for specifically religious initiatives."

Faith has enabled the members of the HPCC to hang on long after pure obstinacy would have run out. It helps them to look at success and failure in a different way. "When I look at Bridge Park with the natural eye I feel depressed, angry, hurt, used, weak; I feel I've had enough," says Williams. "When I look at it from God's perspective, I feel completely different. I see the fulfillment of the dream we once had; I see people being educated, trained, feeling fulfilled in their lives, being successful, being able to unleash their unlimited potential. And then I say to myself, I'm going on."

In spite of the present difficulties, there have been real achievements. Where there were two black businesses in Harlesden High

P. Carr

Lawrence Fearon: "there are people who wouldn't have a job or a home without Bridge Park"

Street when they began, there are now at least twenty, according to Brown. The area is now a major development area, drawing millions of pounds, and the HPCC helped put it on the map. And although Bridge Park itself is struggling, some of its off-shoots are thriving. SCoLAR, set up by Williams, runs training programs for the long-term unemployed and in schools and prisons; it also contributes to the training of civil servants and prison governors. The HPCC has played a part in setting up numerous enterprises.

Individually, each of the men is involved in helping other communities, at home and abroad, to launch their own projects.

Wilson and Fearon both work for Christian organizations involved in social issues; Brown works with the London Enterprise Board, helping young people set up businesses; Johnson is an international consultant. The future, says Wilson, "has got to be about how the principles we have acquired here are replicated elsewhere."

They miss the early days, before the hassles of administration and grant raising took them away from the hands-on work with the community. Was Bridge Park a mistake?

"I would not say I wish I had not done it," reflects Fearon. "We had the experience of working through a vision and seeing something of it come to fruition. We can point to it as an example. There are people who wouldn't have had a job or a home without Bridge Park, and that makes it all worthwhile." He believes that the HPCC made mistakes in allowing itself to become a political football and in failing to organize local support. "If I did it again," he says, "I'd be a lot more astute."

Notes

1. Martin Clark, "Inner City, Inner Person" (dissertation, Girton College, Cambridge, 1988).
2. Clark, "Inner City, Inner Person" (figures from 1981 census).
3. The account of the HPCC is drawn from interviews with Delaney Brown, Lawrence Fearon, Richard Gutch, Leonard Johnson, Errol Williams, Mike Wilson, and Charles Wood. See also Mike Lowe, "The Builders of Brent," *For a Change*, April 1988; Paul Williams, *It Can Be Done* (London: n.p., 1992).

Building Bridges in Bradford

Nearly 200 years ago, the textile mills of Bradford, Yorkshire, stood at the hub of the revolution that transformed Britain from an agrarian society to an industrial one. Today the city is one of the anvils on which another equally historic development is being hammered out: the transformation of Britain from a comparatively monocultural society to a multicultural one.

Some 15 percent of Bradford's population, and 25 percent of its schoolchildren, have South Asian origins.[1] One in nine of its people are Muslims from South Asia, a higher percentage than in any other British city. Bradford calls itself the "curry capital" of Britain,[2] and Muslims have referred to it as the country's "Islamabad" or "city of Islam."[3] It was the first city in Britain to have an Asian lord mayor.

Bradford's Muslim population has placed it on the front line of relations between the Islamic world and the West. Community leaders in Bradford spearheaded British Muslims' campaign against Salman Rushdie's book *The Satanic Verses* and their opposition to British and U.S. intervention in the Persian Gulf. "No city was more important in the construction of a British Muslim identity," writes Philip Lewis, adviser on interfaith issues to the Anglican bishop of Bradford.[4]

In spite of a thriving Asian business sector, the city mirrors many of the problems facing ethnic minorities in Britain today—disproportionate unemployment, underachievement at school, youth gangs, isolation from one another and from the majority community. But it has also demonstrated the ability of people of different faiths to work together on issues precious to them and to keep the peace on the city's streets.

Bradford's mills have acted as a magnet for immigration since the 1820s. Catholic Irish hand weavers and combers and German merchants, many of them Jewish, came in the nineteenth century; Poles, Ukrainians, and Italians came in the 1940s. The first Asians began to arrive in the 1950s to work on the buses and in the mills, which were looking for men who would do "women's work" on night shifts, where female labor was banned by law.

The migrants, at first Hindus and Sikhs and later Muslims, were young men who planned to earn their fortunes and return home. One member of a family or a village would follow another in a process of chain migration that had as much to do with the kudos to be gained by sending a son overseas as with the desire to escape poverty.

In 1961, only eighty-one of the 3,376 Pakistanis living in Bradford were women.[5] Then, in 1962 and again in 1971, the British government clamped down on the free entry of Commonwealth citizens. This led to a surge in immigration to "beat the ban" and forced male migrants to decide whether they wanted to go home or to stay in the country and have their families join them. In the 1970s, Bradford's Asian population grew by some 3,000 a year,[6] and by 1981, 11 percent of the city's schoolchildren were of Asian origin.[7]

At the time of the 1991 census, 62,000 people of Asian origin lived in Bradford. Some 49,000 were Muslims from Pakistan and Bangladesh, and most of the rest were Hindus and Sikhs from India. They come from distinct areas: "You can stand on three hillsides in North Pakistan and see the area from which most of Bradford's Pakistani community comes," says David Jackson, the first coordinator of Bradford's Interfaith Education Centre (IFEC). Over half the city's Muslims have roots in villages near Mirpur in Pakistan, which were flooded to create the Mangla Dam in the early 1960s.[8]

Families and former neighbors clustered together in the inner city, close to their jobs. Over the years, the more successful moved out to the suburbs, especially from the Hindu and Sikh communities. But in 1991, two-thirds of Bradford's South Asians still lived in four inner-city electoral wards.[9] These communities have been hard hit by recession and the decline in manufacturing. Between 1961 and 1991, Bradford's textile industries eliminated 61,000 jobs. The Asian communities, which provided 8 percent of Bradford's workforce but 20 percent of its textile workers, were the most adversely affected.[10] In 1991, the unemployment rate for Asians in Bradford stood at almost 30 percent, compared with 9 percent for the white majority.[11]

Over the last decade, Bradford has seen a shift in its perception of minority identities. In the early 1980s, race-relations workers labored under "a fiction of unitary black identity," according to Philip Lewis. This ignored the myriad dissimilarities among people from different countries in Africa, the West Indies, and Asia, to say nothing of those from different parts of the same country. In these circumstances, religion provides a more useful and acceptable source of identification.

In a city with five *gurdwaras* (Sikh temples), four Hindu temples, and some forty mosques and Islamic schools, many belonging to rival denominations, religion can be divisive. "Historically, these are faith communities who have been at one another's throats," says Ishtiaq Ahmed, director of the Bradford Racial Equality Council (REC). "If you look at any conflict around the globe, one or two are involved. For these communities to come to any kind of common understanding is not easy." Conflicts overseas can have explosive repercussions in Bradford. And there is resentment among the smaller minority communities at the Muslims' growing political power and influence within the city.

But in an increasingly secular society, faith can also be a rallying point across religious differences. "We are all trying to preserve our faith identity against a growing secular threat," says Ishtiaq Ahmed. Friendships forged in the early 1980s, around the issue of the place of religion in schools, have enabled the communities to come together at times of crisis.

For Bradford's South Asian population, religion is an integral part of life. Explains Ishtiaq Ahmed, "It is what we are, our identity, the way we live, see things, do things. You can't place it in one corner." Concern that Britain's state schools were side-lining faith—and with it the identities of children from Asian backgrounds—spurred Bradford's education debate in the 1980s. "The Muslim community was saying that the current secular school environment was not conducive to Muslim children learning about Islam, seeing their faith in a positive light, and making it an integral part of their identity," says Ahmed.

Bradford's inspector for religious education, David Jackson, first came to the city in 1976 to teach at a secondary school with a growing population of Muslims and Hindus. He says, "The basic principle of religious education in those days was to nurture children in Christianity—it was assumed that that was what they were. It was still largely a question of Bible stories. People were beginning to say that this was not enough. In 1982, it dawned on the people of Bradford that in terms of equal opportunities, religious education was in need of revision."

By law, each education authority in Britain had the power to draw up its own religious education (RE) syllabus at a conference of representatives of the different denominations and faiths in the area. The job of convening the conference on Bradford's RE syllabus fell to the local religious education adviser for schools, Brenda Thomson. She was particularly well suited for the task: she was a teacher and a Baptist with experience in racism awareness and peace work, and she had a multiracial family of her own and many contacts in the South Asian communities.

The syllabus had to be agreed to by four committees—one representing the area's teachers; one representing the local government and education authority; a third representing the state church, the Church of England; and a fourth representing all the other denominations and faiths in the area. The syllabus could not be implemented unless every committee voted for it.

P. Carr

Ishtiaq Ahmed, director of the Bradford Racial Equality Council: "you can't place religion in one corner"

Thomson realized that if she ensured that the minority groups held the majority on the fourth committee, they would have equal footing with the Church of England.

The conference's achievement was to shift the syllabus away from nurturing and instructing children in one particular faith—which, says Jackson, "is no longer the role of the school"—toward a wider perspective. "What emerged was an agreement among people of faith that RE in the city schools was about bringing pupils to an equality of respect for different beliefs through understanding and knowing about different religions."

The process was not without its conflicts. Some Christians found it hard to give up the concept of Christian nurture, and the Muslims were suspicious of their intentions. The Muslims walked out of the first meeting in November 1982. Brenda Thomson reassured them that the concept of religious education had no place for proselytization and persuaded them to return.

"We managed to get agreement on two points: that we all loved our children, and that the school system was selling them short on the spiritual dimension," she says. The meetings continued for nine months and included a residential weekend. To Thomson's surprise, the conservative evangelical Christians and the Muslims got on well. Initially, "they were both of a mind that it was their responsibility to convert the other person, and when they saw that neither was going to budge, they realized that they would have to work together. People began to realize that you can't understand other people by telling them what they believe, and they began to listen to each other. Once the group accepted that there were irreconcilable differences and that they could live with them, we began to move forward."

When it came to the final agreement, the Muslims, led by local businessman Sher Azam, threatened to impose a veto unless the local government provided resources to support the new RE policy. This led to the setting up of the Interfaith Education Centre (IFEC) in 1983, which Sher Azam describes as "a center of light and knowledge for people who have somehow misunderstood faith." Jackson was appointed its first coordinator.

The IFEC acts as a resource center for RE teachers and provides RE assistants from the different communities to advise teachers, act as liaisons with their own communities, and lead single-faith worship in schools that have obtained permission to opt out of the government's ruling that every schoolchild must take part in a daily act of collective worship with a largely Christian bias. The center also offers training for teachers and has embarked on religious and cultural awareness training for other sectors of the community, including hospital workers and police.

Its public funding, multifaith nature, and RE assistants—all people with a real commitment to their own faith—make IFEC unique in Britain. Sharin Hussain, one of the IFEC's Muslim RE assistants, believes that her work is essential to building up Muslim children's self-esteem. "When I was young and in school in Bradford, I was ashamed to be a Muslim," she says. "I wished I was a Christian." Her presence in the schools helps to educate not only Muslim children but the others as well. "At certain times of the year I take mixed assemblies," she says. "Children come

M. Smith

David Jackson, first coordinator of Bradford's Interfaith Education Centre: "bringing an equality of respect for different beliefs"

up and talk to me in the street afterwards—they have discovered that I am normal, in spite of the fact that I dress differently from them."

Parallel to the RE debate, the Bradford education authority also took steps to make schools more sensitive to Muslim dietary and clothing requirements. In 1984, after a campaign by the city's Muslims that was supported by the Anglican community-relations chaplain, Bradford became the first authority to provide *halal* meat (meat from animals that have been killed according to Islamic law) in its schools.

These policies provoked a right-wing backlash in 1984 around the case of Ray Honeyford, the headmaster of a predominantly Muslim school who maintained that efforts to accommodate minority needs were undermining social cohesion and penalizing white children. The issues, according to Philip Lewis, were never seriously debated, "with the headmaster demonized by the left as a racist and lionized by the right as a doughty defender of free speech."[12] But Honeyford's disparaging remarks offended all the ethnic minorities. Eventually, in 1985, Honeyford was persuaded to take early retirement.

The friendships built up over education have had their spin-offs in interfaith relations. When sixty-four spectators died in a fire at the city's football stadium in 1985, representatives of all Bradford's faiths took part in the memorial service. Three years later, when South Africa's Archbishop Desmond Tutu preached at the rebuilt grounds to 10,000 people, all the city's religious communities took part in the service, whose theme was justice. And in 1991, the city's newspaper, the *Bradford Telegraph and Argus*, replaced its Saturday religious slot, which had been written by local Christians for seventy years, with a new column written by people from all the city's faiths.

In early 1989, twelve Muslims and Christians from Bradford went on a three-week trip to Pakistan sponsored by the Columban Fathers, a Catholic order oriented toward justice and peace issues. The idea was for Bradford Christians and Muslims to experience "the reverse mirror" of Britain in a country where Muslims were in the majority. Among the four Muslims who acted as hosts for the trip was Ishtiaq Ahmed; David Jackson, Philip Lewis, and a local teacher, Mollie Somerville, were among the Christians. Both faith groups included different denominations. They visited the areas that the pioneers of Bradford's Pakistani community had come from and stayed with local families.

"We learned as much about our own faith and the differences within our faith as we did about other people's," says Mollie Somerville. For instance, whereas the Catholics in the group responded positively to the shrines of Muslim Sufis that they visited, some of the Protestants and Muslims did not. "The group divided not between Muslims and Christians but between those who could accept this kind of worship and those who could not."

"I became a better Muslim as a result of the trip," says Ishtiaq Ahmed. "It gave me a chance too to have a real insight into the Christian faith. As we prepared for the trip and then lived and traveled together, often in very trying circumstances, we became friends."

One friendship that had practical results was that between Mollie Somerville and Nighat Mirza, headteacher of Bradford's independent Muslim Girls' Community School (now Feversham College). Upon their return, Mirza asked Somerville to teach French part time at the school and later, when the school began to enter pupils for state exams in religious studies, to teach the Christian component of the course.

Two videos have also resulted: *Barriers or Bridges?* which tells the story of the journey to Pakistan and the attempts of Muslims and Christians to work together in Bradford, and *Call to Prayer: Call to Partnership*, which looks at what faith means to the poorest of the poor in Pakistan, focusing on a Christian community and a Muslim one. Their aim, explains Ishtiaq Ahmed, is to offer something of what the travelers discovered to a wider audience.

The strength of the alliance between Bradford's faith communities has also been tested by more contentious issues. The most notorious of these was the *Satanic Verses* affair in 1988–89.

Bradford's Council for Mosques, founded in 1981, has been described as "probably the most representative voice of Islam in the land."[13] With two delegates from each of Bradford's forty Islamic institutions, it spans the city's different Muslim denominations and meets once a year to discuss issues affecting them. Between meetings, its president and his executive team act on its behalf. For almost half of its first decade, its president was Sher Azam, described by Brenda Thomson as "an amazingly talented negotiator, a peaceful and wise person."

Sher Azam sees faith as fundamental: "It tells us where we come from and where we go. Living without faith is like reading a book and skipping the first and last chapters." He took the lead when news first reached Bradford's Muslims that Salman Rushdie's book contained material that was offensive to Islam. The Council for Mosques' campaign, which culminated in the burning of a copy of the book in January 1989, earned Bradford unjustified notoriety as a hotbed of fundamentalism and thrust Sher Azam and his colleagues into the national spotlight.

To Sher Azam, the book burning was a last resort, after a series of letters to the publishers, politicians, and the British government brought derisory responses. "We wanted to draw these people's attention to the fact that the book would cause problems," he says. "We hoped that at least the government would call a meeting of Muslims to hear our point of view. By December, all our avenues were closing. We felt that we were being abused and that it would become acceptable to insult Islam." He has continued to campaign for a change in Britain's blasphemy laws to protect all faiths, or for an extension to the mainland of a Northern Irish law against incitement to religious hatred.

The issue went beyond the book itself to the wider issue of Muslims' right to be heard in their own country of citizenship. "Muslims were saying that we have been here for forty years; many of us were born and brought up here," says Ishtiaq Ahmed. "Can we ask for a degree of protection to ensure that our faith values are not abused and that we can live here in respect and dignity, second to none?"

In attacking the *Satanic Verses*, and asking for it to be withdrawn, Bradford's Muslims were challenging "what has been held in Britain as most sacred—freedom of expression and creativity," says Ishtiaq Ahmed. The book burning and Iran's death sentence against Rushdie—which few Bradford Muslims supported—opened the floodgates to a "deluge of anti-Islamic sentiment," says Lewis. The accusations of "fundamentalism" that filled the press reflected "a worrying failure of the secular imagination to understand a religious tradition, one might almost say any religious tradition."[14]

At this time of crisis, Bradford's different faith communities— particularly Anglican bishop Robert Williamson—rallied to the Muslims' support. Williamson appealed to the publishers to reconsider the distribution of the book, urged British society to take the Muslims' views seriously, and organized meetings among Bradford's Muslims, civic leaders, politicians, and police on the issues raised by the affair. He also urged Muslim leaders to avoid counterproductive actions.[15]

The outbreak of the Gulf War in 1991 once again strained the relationship between communities. "As far as the English were concerned, Saddam was a mad demon, and every decent member of the international community should support America and Britain against him," says Ishtiaq Ahmed. "The view of Muslims in general was that it was an internal Middle Eastern war and that the Middle Eastern countries should come together to find an internal solution."

In this situation, Bradford's faith communities acted as mediators, urging the view that although differences of opinion were legitimate, violent expression of these differences was not. Bishop Williamson called in the church press for sensitivity to Muslim attitudes and described his discussions with Muslim leaders since the invasion of Kuwait. Frank speaking on both sides, he said, was "only possible because relationships of trust have been built up over the years."[16]

In December 1992, militant Hindus tore down the sixteenth-century Babri mosque in Ayodhya, India. Within hours of the news, a Hindu temple in Bradford was firebombed and three Hindu businesses were attacked. By the end of the week, several temples in Britain had been vandalized, and intercommunal violence in India had claimed over a thousand lives.[17]

For Bradford, says Ishtiaq Ahmed, the crisis was a test of ten years of relationship building. "Emotions were very high. The REC approached the bishop's office and the Council for Mosques, and we were able to convene an almost immediate meeting of the faith communities." By the evening after the Ayodhya attack, he was able to release a joint statement by Hindu, Muslim, Sikh, and Christian leaders, condemning the violence.[18] Later, council leaders and leaders of the faith communities met in the Hindu temple that had been attacked. The fact that Mus-lims and Hindus met together in a Hindu temple was historic enough in itself, but they also agreed that if need be, they would stand guard to protect each other's places of worship from people of their own communities. "Something like that doesn't just happen," Ahmed asserts. "It was a result of the close ties built during those early years around education."

Those seeking to build bridges in Bradford face daunting odds. Not only are the minority communities disadvantaged in comparison with the majority, but they are deeply divided among themselves. "Interaction between various communities is small and generally superficial," writes Ramindar Singh, head of the Department of Contemporary Studies at Bradford and Ilkley Community College and a former deputy chairman of the Commission for Racial Equality. "The community leaders generally talk about developing solidarity, a wonderful notion and a powerful tool to use for obtaining their full rights of citizenship in their new home. But, so far, it appears an unachievable objective."[19]

In spite of this, Singh acknowledges that the "cordial relationship" among the leaders of the city's religious organizations has contributed to the "development and maintenance of tolerant attitudes by Bradford's entire population, including the minority communities."[20]

Over the last decade, the trust established among the leaders of Bradford's different faiths has enabled them to address common issues of concern and to act as mediators and troubleshooters in the community. The challenge now is to find ways of transmitting this common acceptance and understanding to believers, and nonbelievers, on the street.

Notes

This chapter is drawn from my interviews in November 1994 with Ishtiaq Ahmed, Sher Azam, David Bowen, David Jackson, and religious education assistants at Bradford's Interfaith Education Centre, Philip Lewis, Mollie Somerville, and Brenda Thomson. See also Michael Smith's articles in *For a Change* (October 1988, January 1990).

1. Philip Lewis, "Beyond Babel: An Anglican Perspective in Bradford" (Eighth Lambeth Interfaith Lecture, London, November 17, 1992).
2. Ramindar Singh, introduction to *Here to Stay: Bradford's South Asian Communities* (Bradford: City of Bradford Metropolitan Council, 1994).

3. Philip Lewis, *Islamic Britain: Religion, Politics and Identity Among British Muslims* (London: I. B. Tauris, 1994).

4. Lewis, *Islamic Britain*, 4.

5. Lewis, *Islamic Britain*.

6. Singh, introduction.

7. Lewis, *Islamic Britain*.

8. Singh, introduction.

9. Singh, introduction.

10. Lewis, *Islamic Britain*.

11. Singh, introduction.

12. Lewis, "Beyond Babel."

13. Mihir Bose, *The Sunday Telegraph*, January 5, 1992, quoted in Lewis, *Islamic Britain*, 143.

14. Lewis, "Beyond Babel."

15. Simon Lee and Peter Stanford, *Believing Bishops* (London: Faber and Faber, 1990).

16. *The Church of England Newspaper*, January 25, 1991.

17. *Yorkshire on Sunday*, December 13, 1992.

18. *Yorkshire Post*, December 8, 1992.

19. Singh, introduction, 14.

20. Singh, introduction, 20.

CHAPTER 10

Atlanta: The Fight
for Survival

As a black teenager living in the American city of
Atlanta, Georgia, in 1990, fifteen-year-old Ron
Sailor Jr. was more likely to be shot than to reach his twenty-
fifth birthday. That year he attended the funerals of seven of his
contemporaries.[1]

Every day across the United States, an average of fourteen
teenagers and children die of gunshot wounds.[2] The National
Education Association estimated in July 1993 that 100,000
young Americans take guns to school.[3] Although the number
of Americans between ages ten and seventeen has declined by
over 10 percent since the mid-1980s, violent juvenile crime has
risen by about 10 percent.[4] Los Angeles alone averaged almost
three gang-related murders every day in 1992.[5]

The vast majority of the victims and perpetrators of these
crimes are young African American men. In the early 1990s,
homicide was the leading cause of death for African Americans between the ages of fifteen and twenty-four.[6] Such figures
led the first African American to be elected state governor,
Douglas Wilder of Virginia, to tell a Senate committee in 1991
that the country's young black men were a "disappearing generation."[7] About a quarter of all African American men in their
twenties were behind bars, on parole, or on probation, he said.
Three years earlier, Benjamin Hooks, executive director of the
National Association for the Advancement of Colored People
(NAACP), had given an even grimmer warning. By the year
2012, he said, 70 percent of black men who were between

eighteen and twenty-seven in 1988 would be on drugs, in jail, or dead.[8]

The causes are numerous: lack of jobs—48 percent of black male teenagers were unemployed in the last quarter of 1990;[9] the rise of gangs—Los Angeles alone has some 100,000 gang members;[10] the breakdown in family life and the absence of father figures—nearly two-thirds of black children are born out of wedlock, and the majority live with their mothers only;[11] the availability of drugs, alcohol, and guns. *Time* reckons that there are 67 million privately owned handguns in the United States, more than one for every four Americans of all ages.[12] Urban deprivation plays a part too, though some of the most violent schools are middle class.

As state and city governments, police, teachers, churches, and youth workers struggle to control the problem, a group of young black men in Atlanta has decided to take their fate into their own hands. Ron Sailor and his colleagues have refused to be written off as an "endangered species." In 1989, they launched their own bid to outlaw teen violence in their city. Since then, according to the Atlanta police, their organization—Black Teens for Advancement (BTA)—has cut the violence in Atlanta's public schools by 57 percent.[13]

Fifty-four percent of Central Atlanta's population, and 97 percent of its school population, is black. Benjamin E. Mays School, a predominantly middle-class high school with some 1,500 pupils, has only four or five white students. "We are the only school in the city that has been chosen as a national school of excellence twice," says social studies teacher Edward Johnson. "But racist attitudes are such that whites would rather send their children to an inferior school that's white than to a superior one that's black."

Kids at Mays—and in Atlanta's other schools—used to see fighting as a sort of sport, according to Floyd Wood II, "executive spokesman" of BTA in 1993–94, when he was fifteen. Sporting events provided flash points for interschool battles, and fighting spilled over into the city's transit system and restaurants. The authorities had tried to address the issue by sending athletes and other adult role models to speak in the schools, but without success.

The idea of BTA was born at a basketball game at Mays in January 1989, says Feiji McKay, one of the founders. "Someone found the courage to ask, almost rhetorically, 'Why are we doing all this fighting? It's senseless. We're fighting over hats and jackets. I can't even go to the mall and buy a pair of sneakers without fearing for my life.' It takes a lot of courage to ask a question like that among your peers, people whose mind-set is 'so and so did this, I think it's time to roll over there and get them.' That may have stopped someone from getting hurt that day."

The students decided to invite their main rival, Douglass High, to a meeting to talk about how to stop the violence. "Initially, the Douglass students saw the invitation as a setup," says McKay. But instead of the expected six, fifty-three turned up. They pledged themselves to stand against violence on school premises. "Then they went back and talked to others—it was like spontaneous combustion."

The meeting led to an immediate decline in local violence, writes another of the founders, Kwanza Hall. Social functions at both schools took place peacefully the next weekend. "This was a landmark event for the city of Atlanta because these two schools, even though mainly middle-class in makeup, had the highest problem of violence in the entire Atlanta public schools system."[14]

The next week, 132 students turned up at the meeting, and a third school was represented. For the next three months, the students targeted a new school every week. As a result, maintained Walter F. Collier of the Atlanta Department of Public Safety, crime and violence within the school system fell by 40 percent.

By May, seventeen schools and a thousand students were involved. By 1994, the numbers had built to over 5,000. Chapters had opened in six other cities in Minnesota, Virginia, and Washington State, as well as in Georgia. BTA had been honored by the Southern Christian Leadership Conference, the NAACP, and the governor of Georgia.

BTA used the teens' social grapevine to spread messages and rally people for meetings. When a local drug dealer invited all Atlanta's public school teenagers to a Christmas party with free alcohol, BTA discovered that "some brothers planned to shoot some other brothers at what was supposed to be a peaceful event." They tagged the party "death at the door" and put the word out to avoid it. Only five teenagers turned up at the party, instead of the expected 300.

Similarly, when Los Angeles plunged into violence in April 1992, BTA passed the word around the schools to cool it. "The brothers had a feeling that if the police who had beaten Rodney King were acquitted there were going to be riots," says Floyd Wood. "So the guys called on each school to have an assembly and talk about what might happen if a riot took place in Atlanta. What violence did occur in Atlanta was downtown, and it was older people, not teenagers from high school. We try to defuse the bomb before it explodes."

Later that year, BTA experienced a setback when the school system canceled BTA's congressional assembly, an event that had drawn 2,500 in 1989, 1990, and 1991 without any violent incidents. The authorities were afraid that the 1992 meeting might erupt into violence, as a non-BTA gathering of some 3,000 students had a few weeks before. "It's like some of these adults in high places don't want to see black male teenagers coming together in unity," says Wood. But, he adds philosophically, the cancellation gave BTA a chance to concentrate on the buildup of tension between two school-based gangs that could have led to a bloodbath. BTA persuaded the two gangs to meet together, and they buried the hatchet.

BTA's secret of success appears to have been that it offers young men a way to break out of the cycle of violence without losing face. From the beginning, they have banned both adults and girls from their meetings, because young men tend to clam up in front of the former and show off in front of the latter. They have created a nonviolent in-group that provides an alternative to the gangs.

P. Carr

BTA members at an international conference: defusing the bomb before it explodes

"People were just waiting for an initiative like this," explains McKay. "Most of them had long since stopped enjoying the endless gang wars, the fear, not knowing if they'd come out alive this time. But getting out was uncool. When the leaders of the two best known gangs got reconciled, the rest could follow."

It helped that BTA's founders were known to be hard men, not teachers' pets. Kwanza Hall, who went on to study at MIT, was "a little godfather," according to a teacher at his school. Feiji McKay describes his former self as "an undercover thug." Other leaders included the mastermind behind the frequent outbreaks of fighting at the city's rapid-transit station and a drug pusher who had twice been injured in shooting incidents. "A lot of the architects of BTA were the same people who had orchestrated the violence between the schools," says McKay.

Like many others, Jamal Tandy followed his role models into BTA. "When my cousins went fighting, I was always trailing right behind them," he says. "At Mays I was seen as a problem student, the sort who causes chaos. Then my cousins started changing and telling me, 'Chill out, this isn't the thing to do.' That really kind of got at me to go to BTA." Now he is seen "as a student who solves problems."

"I saw a lot of friends fight, get shot and beaten up, and I feared that one day I might be in that situation," says Floyd Wood. "I would go to people in the church, but they weren't very effective. I got tired of getting calls late at night saying 'so and so just got beat up.' The media fuels the violence by portraying black male teenagers as savage beasts who just go out killing and shooting, but it is not true."

BTA gets kids off the streets, but it also teaches social skills. Encountered at an international conference, its leaders are dressed in suits. They have their cards at the ready, emblazoned with their official titles. "I feel BTA is going to prepare me for life," says Wood. "I'm learning how to use the right fork, to conduct a formal meeting, to give an interview. It's a way to get out of danger. It's almost like college."

The organization has a markedly religious tone and includes both Christians and Muslims. New recruits accept the "BTA creed of brotherhood": "I, being a young black man, do understand that it is my duty to uphold all standards of BTA. I must remain strong and never do wrong, for if I do, it not only hurts me, but also my fellow brothers. I represent my brother and he represents me: therefore everything I do and say represents all brothers of BTA. I am black, I am proud, and I am at peace with my brother."

They also adopt the "teen commandments," which include injunctions to think before drinking, to choose friends carefully, not to follow the crowd or show off when driving, and to go to public worship. "Or even better," asserts number ten, "keep the original Ten Commandments."

The group has been criticized for the use of "black" in its title. It insists that it doesn't discriminate—all races, including whites, are welcome—but that it is young black men who are most at risk. It is adamant, too, about its no-women, no-adults rule. A sister organization has been set up, GIRLS (Generating Integrity, Responsibility, Leadership and Service) Unlimited.

Edward Johnson, the only adult allowed into their meetings, believes that they've got their age threshold right. He grew up on the streets himself, eating out of trash cans until an aunt took him in hand; he has taught teenagers for over thirty-five years. He sees his role as a "father at a distance," providing backup and continuity as generations pass in and out of high school and BTA. "If I take over just once, I give people the chance to say 'it's just that teacher.'"

"Mr Johnson is the type of adult we need more of," says Floyd Wood. "But if he gets up in a meeting, we say, 'Sit down, Mr. Johnson, this is our meeting now.'"

Johnson's seems a somewhat thankless task, on top of his job, extensive church commitments, and family life. He admits that it is "rough, tiring, trying, taxing, and demanding. But it's easier than going to trials, hospitals, funerals and trying to correct wrecked lives when it's too late. I got sick and tired of listening and watching grown folk talk about the problem and not do anything." His biggest job has been preventing the boys from being used by people with political interests.

Feiji McKay, now out of school and working for the postal service to earn money for college tuition, still takes part in BTA missions, when invited. He dreams of setting up a veterans' branch and a "complete cascade of organizations down to kindergarten level."

Portia Scott, editor of the *Atlanta Daily World*, the oldest black daily newspaper in the United States, believes that BTA is unique and long overdue. "Atlanta is a very high-crime city," she says. "We've lost a lot of young people to violence. We had got to the point where young people really didn't have any respect for other people anymore. BTA is turning some of that around, by reaching out to their peers. Anyone can join, from a high-income family or a lower one, and find a leadership role and a sense of family and self-esteem."

BTA's main area of success has been cutting violence on school premises. By 1993, BTA had been going for four years, and violent crime in Atlanta as a whole had risen by nearly 300 percent over the last five years.[15] No one was claiming that BTA could do the job by itself or that its success had been total. But for a significant number of young men, it had offered an alternative to crime and fighting. "The point is that we do save some of them," says Wood. "We do save some lives."

Notes

The account of BTA is taken from my interviews with Feiji McKay, Jamal Tandy, Floyd Wood, Edward Johnson, and George and Bernice Lemon in August 1993 and from BTA literature and reports supplied by them. See also Nancy Creach's profile of Edward Johnson in *For a Change* (October 1991).

1. *Richmond Times Dispatch*, January 14, 1991.
2. *The Observer*, September 19, 1993.
3. *The Independent Magazine*, September 11, 1993.
4. *The Oregonian*, January 29, 1993.
5. *The Christian Science Monitor*, April 1, 1993.
6. *The Atlanta Journal-Constitution*, April 14, 1992.
7. *The Palm Beach Post*, March 20, 1991.
8. *The Atlanta Journal-Constitution*, November 15, 1989.
9. *The Palm Beach Post*, March 20, 1991.
10. *The Christian Science Monitor*, April 1, 1993.
11. UNDP, *Human Development Report, 1993* (New York/Oxford: Oxford University Press, 1993).
12. *Time*, December 20, 1993.
13. *The Atlanta Journal-Constitution*, September 24, 1993.
14. Kwanza Hall, unpublished and undated background paper.
15. *The Christian Science Monitor*, May 11, 1993.

CHAPTER 11

The Three Rs
of Community Development

More Americans live in poverty today than at any time in the last thirty years.[1] Their plight presents not only a material but also a spiritual challenge to American society, according to community development guru John Perkins. "Changing a life or changing a community is ultimately a spiritual issue," he asserts.[2] Born in a poor share-cropping community in Mississippi in 1930, he has earned a global following as an exponent and practitioner of Christian community development.

Like many African Americans of his generation, Perkins fought his way out of poverty. As a boy, he was paid only fifteen cents for a day's farm work; by the time he was thirty, he owned investments and a large house and was well on his way to achieving the American dream. Yet he gave it all up to return to his roots and work with those who had been left behind in the struggle for a better life.

Perkins cites racism, unjust economic structures, middle-class flight, and misguided welfare programs as the major forces behind urban poverty in America today. Racist attitudes make whites "look at inner cities, see black or brown, and label the problem 'not my fault' and 'not my responsibility.'" Slavery has left blacks with a "deflated sense of self" that can paralyze their will to achieve.[3] Neither power nor wealth are fairly distributed. In 1979, blacks owned only 2 percent of the nation's assets, although they made up over 10 percent of the population.[4] And although there are ten times as many black office-holders in eight southern states today as there were twenty years ago,[5] power is still largely a white commodity.

According to one survey, two-thirds of black Americans enjoy comfortable lifestyles today, compared with only a sixth in 1950. Two-thirds of black adults had completed high school in 1988; less than a quarter had in 1960.[6] Education, economic advancement, and the removal of racist housing laws have swung open the gates of the ghetto for those who can afford to escape. This progress has had a downside for inner-city community life, Perkins believes.

In the bad old days of segregation, the professional classes were "the stablizing glue" that held communities together, Perkins explains. "The exodus of their families, their skills and their daily civic and moral leadership hastened the unraveling of the inner city, leaving a vacuum of leadership."[7]

Young Americans growing up in the inner cities have few opportunities to fight their way out of the poverty trap and few role models to prove that it can be done. The welfare system, Perkins maintains, only makes things worse. Programs designed to help single mothers have acted as a disincentive toward marriage and stability. Young women are trapped in a system "where the easiest way to get more money is to have more kids";[8] young men find it easier and more profitable "to sell drugs or to live off their girlfriends' welfare cheques" than to work for an inadequate minimum wage.[9] For many young people, gangs offer the sense of belonging that is lacking at home.

He compares today's black urban youth to "powder kegs: without the disciplines of strong families or community, constantly told by society that materialism makes life worthwhile, perceiving middle-class Americans as having everything they can't have, seeing police as just another gang out to get them."[10]

In response to this analysis, Perkins urges community workers to adopt a three-point agenda: relocation, reconciliation, and redistribution. This is no ivory-tower theorum but the fruit of a painful spiritual journey that has taken him from atheism to faith and extended his horizons from the sufferings of his own race to the need for healing in all communities.

Perkins was born in New Hebron, Mississippi—still America's poorest state today.[11] His mother was suffering from protein deficiency when he was born and died when he was seven months old. His father left home. John and his elder brother were brought up by their grandmother, and their three siblings were sent to live with other relations.

The extended Perkins family made its living by sharecropping, bootlegging, and running gambling dens. By the time John was sixteen, he had attended the funerals of his sister, who had been murdered by her boyfriend, and of his brother, who had died in his arms after being shot by the town's marshal in a racist attack. He dropped out of school for two years between the ages of twelve and fourteen and quit altogether when he was fifteen. By then, he had discovered that a black person could not expect any justice in the white man's world of the Deep South.

After his brother's murder, the family was afraid that John might take the law into his own hands, so he was packed off to relatives in California. He found work in the Union Pacific Foundry in South Gate, became active in the United Steel Workers' Union, and led a successful strike—all while still in his teens. He married Vera Mae in 1951, spent two years in the army during the Korean War, and returned to set up home in Monrovia, California. By 1960, he had five children, was rising in a good job, and owned stock and property. He felt that he was beginning to achieve his goals.

In 1957, however, something had happened that was to overturn his agenda. His four-year-old son, Spencer, started going to a Bible class at a local church and kept asking Perkins to go with him. Although Vera Mae was a Christian, Perkins had always rejected the church as an instrument of white oppression and a vehicle for black emotionalism. Since his marriage, however, he had been searching for "something deeper and greater in life" and had had brief involvements with the Jehovah's Witnesses and Scientology.

M. Brown

John Perkins: relocation, reconciliation, and redistribution

Something about the Bible classes seemed to be making Spencer happier, so Perkins eventually gave in and went along. He also agreed to go to church with a friend from work. He was impressed by the warmth and sincerity of the black Christians he met and began to read the Bible. The figure of St. Paul particularly caught his imagination: he recognized someone who was as highly motivated as he was, but by something more than his own economic betterment.

One Sunday morning in church, several months after he had started reading the Bible, things fell into place for Perkins. "I discovered that God loved me," he writes. "I grew up without the certainty of love. That morning all the longings of my heart came together. . . . In the midst of all my feelings of inferiority, in spite of the fact that I was a third-grade dropout, at the age of twenty-seven I reached out to God. It seemed that this was the morning that I had been born for."[12]

Perkins's conversion spurred him into theological study, evangelical work, and, ultimately, social action. He joined a group of Christian businessmen on a mission to a prison camp and found

that many of the young inmates came from southern backgrounds just like his but had failed to make good in California.
He saw that many of the problems of the ghetto "were really the
unsolved problems of the South I had left. I couldn't escape a
conviction . . . that God wanted me back in Mississippi, to identify with my people there, to help them break up the cycle of
despair—not by encouraging them to leave, but by showing them
new life right where they were."[13]

It took two years for the Perkinses to decide to leave the good
life they were establishing in California and return to Mississippi. They moved to the black section of the town of Mendenhall
and started out by running Bible schools for children and young
people. Gradually, the community's needs drew them into social
programs and civil rights work, in the face of opposition
from the white community and authorities and from some black
Christians. They were harassed by the Ku Klux Klan and by the
police. Finally, in February 1970, Perkins was arrested with a
group of young people and nearly beaten to death.

The experience had a surprising impact on Perkins's approach
to community work. Until then, he writes, "what I really wanted
was for the white man to leave us alone." The assault might
have been expected to reinforce this desire, but instead, Perkins
emerged with a determination to "take a gospel of love to whites
filled with hate."

The beating, he writes, showed him what hatred could do to
people. "These policemen were poor. They saw themselves as
failures. The only way they knew how to find a sense of worth
was by beating us." Unable to hate them, he had prayed, "God,
if you will let me get out of this jail alive, I really want to preach
a gospel that will heal these people too."[14]

After the assault, and under the stress of trying to win justice
from the biased, white-controlled legal system, Perkins's health
broke down, forcing him to spend several weeks in the hospital
in the summer of 1970 and the spring of 1971. Lying there, he
wrestled again with his bitterness at all he and his people had
suffered at the hands of whites who called themselves Christians.
"I began to think there was only one way to go—to give up on

whites and white Christians and just work for me and mine."
But he was unable to escape from the imperative to forgive that
was inherent in his Christian faith. As the weeks went by, he
found "a deep inner healing" of the wounds that went back to
his earliest childhood. He emerged with a conviction that reconciliation rather than confrontation was the way forward. "True
justice could come only as people's hearts were made right
with God and God's love motivated them to be reconciled with
one another."[15]

Perkins's return to Mississippi was the beginning of thirty-five
years of work in poor communities in Mississippi and California. He has built up a network of groups in some eighty cities
that are putting his "three Rs of development" into practice in
their communities, under the umbrella of the Christian Community Development Association (CCDA).

He believes that people of faith should get involved in the
fight against poverty, both as individuals and as groups. But he
warns against do-gooding, paternalism, and quick fixes. Developing people is more important than developing programs, he
states, and the true mark of success is when newcomers can hand
authority over to indigenous leaders.

Perkins has preached—and practiced—the first R, relocation,
from his earliest days in community work. Since that first move
from California, he and Vera Mae have lived and brought up
their eight children in the neighborhoods where they worked.
Perkins recognizes that the challenge of relocation is a hard one
for many would-be community workers to swallow, but he
believes that it is vital. Poor people are more likely to trust people
who live among them, he believes. "If you make the community your home, you don't have to walk round saying you're
committed."[16] The need for schools, health care, and security
ceases to be a theory; it becomes your own need as well.

The difference between this form of relocation and gentri-
fication, Perkins asserts, is motive and involvement. It's not a
question of fixing up cheap houses and displacing local people,
but of accepting a lower standard of living and the pressures

of the inner city so as to live alongside the poor. "In most urban areas around the country," he writes, "there is room for hundreds of families to reclaim abandoned neighborhoods." All over America, people of faith, "motivated by their desire to participate in the rebuilding of our inner cities, are sprinkling back in, buying homes, setting down roots and building relationships with unlikely neighbors. They are convinced that their presence is the surest way to begin tackling the problems of their cities."[17] Simply by being there, these people demonstrate to their neighbors that family breakup, crime, and addiction are not inevitable.

Perkins does not dismiss the risks involved in deciding to move into a deprived area. He urges prospective relocators to count the costs before they burn their bridges, to take the time to get proper training and experience, and to work (and ideally move) as part of a group. He describes his own struggle when, shortly after moving back to Mississippi, one of his children got polio. Colleagues in the CCDA have faced repeated burglaries, rape, or assault. Often the crisis point comes when the newcomer has to face up to the true meaning of equal partnership. "I was there to help, to give, to teach and to do," writes Chris Rice, a white community worker in Jackson, Mississippi. "But when the people I said I had come to serve began asking me to be helped, to receive and to learn, that's when I began packing my bags." Like Perkins, Rice eventually unpacked and stayed on.[18]

Relocation also involves stemming the brain and skills drain out of the ghetto into suburbia. During the 1960s, when the Perkinses lived in Mendenhall in Simpson County, 2,210 more black people moved out of the county than moved in—a figure equal to more than a third of its total black population in 1970.[19] Poverty, lack of amenities and jobs, and racism all provided strong incentives for the brightest young people to leave.

From the very beginning, the Perkinses worked on helping young people complete high school, go away to college, and return to work in the community. They set up a day-care center for small children to enable the older brothers and sisters who had been looking after them to return to school. Then they established a tutoring service to help schoolchildren with their studies, a summer school to prepare high school graduates for college, and summer jobs to bring college students back to the community during the long vacation.

By the early 1970s, five local college graduates were back in Mendenhall, running the Voice of Calvary programs that Perkins had begun. "Their love of God had given them a burden to return and heal Mendenhall, rather than to run and escape. The ministeries we had developed had formed an economic base and provided opportunities for employment."[20] Perkins was able to leave things in their hands when, on his doctors' advice, he left the stresses of Mendenhall for Jackson, Mississippi, in 1972. In the years that followed, his successors set up an adult education center, a successful thrift store, and a preschool.

Perkins and his colleagues have set up similar programs in Jackson and in northwest Pasadena, California, where he has lived since 1982. In addition to tutoring, Perkins's Harambee Center in Pasadena aims to offer "parenting" to a community where family life is almost nonexistent. Eighty-four percent of local children have no fathers living with them; one year, only three of the seventy children attending Harambee's after-school tutoring program had both parents at home.[21] The center aims to offer an alternative family to children who might otherwise fall victim to gangs and drug dealers. One of its best contributions to the community, Perkins maintains, has been to provide a space where local children can play basketball.

Since his jail experiences, Perkins's work has emphasized a second R: reconciliation. In 1974, the Perkinses and a white family moved into a six-block area of Jackson that was rapidly turning black, with the aim of becoming a fellowship of blacks and whites ministering to both races. As in Mendenhall, they started out by running Bible classes and then opened a church fellowship, the only place in the city where both races could worship together. As more and more people from outside the area asked to join the church, the Perkinses encouraged them either to move into the area or to join churches in their own neighborhoods.

The fellowship provided a core for the social and economic programs that followed: a housing cooperative, a health center, and a clothing chain that employs thirty-six people. The area also houses the John M. Perkins International Study Center, which trains people from all over America and from the Third World in community development. The population of the neighborhood has now settled at 25 percent white.

In the 1980s, the income gap between the richest and poorest fifths of the population in the United States was higher than in any industrial country except Australia.[22] Perkins's conversion to reconciliation has done nothing to blunt his commitment to the third R, redistribution. Teaching people to fish may fill their plates for longer than simply giving them a fish, but the real issue today, he asserts, is who owns the pond. Back in Mendenhall, he realized that money circulated only twice in the black section of town before returning to the whites, and he set about encouraging cooperatives and black businesses as a means of keeping the money in the community, providing jobs, and offering models of achievement to young people.

Perkins's programs provide on-the-job experience for local young people. In northwest Pasadena, where unemployment is high and the will to work low, he has set up the WorkNet program to teach young people the skills of getting—and keeping—a job. The program also shepherds them through their first six months of employment. As a result, Perkins maintains, most people in the community who want jobs have them. The more difficult job is to inspire those who do not want to work. Hence the importance of "parenting" the local children and encouraging them to realize their potential. More than fifty volunteers from local churches come to Harambee once a week to tutor children one-on-one after school.

Redistribution also involves services and power. Only a tenth of poor pregnant women in America's inner cities receive prenatal care, according to some surveys. Perkins's first attempt at setting up a clinic in Mendenhall was destroyed by a flood in 1974. Voice of Calvary's new health center now stands in the center of town.

Voice of Calvary also runs a health center in Jackson and in Perkins's birthplace, New Hebron. Perkins notes with approval an initiative in Denver, Colorado, where a network of doctors offers free appointments to the urban poor and a prenatal and pediatric clinic is staffed by a roster of volunteer doctors and nurses.

Perkins believes that in the 1990s, empowerment of the poor requires working with the authorities rather than fighting them. He advocates "listening meetings," like those he has pioneered in northwest Pasadena, where city officials can hear from local people. As a veteran of the civil rights movement, he understands the uses of, and need for, confrontation. But, he writes, "I have found in Pasadena that it is not only possible but also desirable to work together with officials. . . . By treating them as friends rather than as enemies, we are able to keep them more accountable to their promises." When it comes to racist or corrupt officials, "we can have a greater influence on the rest of the government to remove these people if we have a good working relationship with the government as a whole."[23]

When John and Vera Mae Perkins returned to southern California in 1982, their plan was retirement rather than further activism. They saw their new home as a haven where Perkins could write and from which he could launch speaking tours.

Then they discovered northwest Pasadena, a five-square-mile area with the highest daytime crime rate in southern California at that time.[24] They couldn't resist moving into the bull's-eye of the ghetto, next door to a major drug outlet. Cars lined up outside to buy, and prostitutes worked in tents in the backyard. Their house was attacked four times in their first year there.

As in Mendenhall and Jackson, they started out by organizing religious activities for the local children. "Our goal," writes Perkins, "was to rescue the children from the environment around them; but it was also to ultimately change the environment they were in."[25] This has begun to happen. Today, the Harambee Center owns the houses that were once drug houses. Other drug outlets have closed down. Children are beginning to venture outside to play. The Perkinses have reclaimed the street.

As crime figures in the ghettos of southern California soar, the Harambee Center is a small oasis in a big desert. All across the United States, similar oases are springing up, linked together by the CCDA. They demonstrate what can be done when people allow their faith to be radical enough to impel them across their comfort and security barriers.

Notes

1. Alan B. Durning, "Ending Poverty," in *State of the World, 1990: Worldwatch Institute Report* (New York: W. W. Norton, 1990).
2. John M. Perkins, *Beyond Charity* (Grand Rapids, Mich.: Baker Books, 1993), 80.
3. Perkins, *Beyond Charity*, 24–25.
4. John M. Perkins, *With Justice for All* (Ventura, Calif.: Regal Books, 1982).
5. *The Oregonian*, August 9, 1992.
6. *The Oregonian*, August 9, 1992.
7. Perkins, *Beyond Charity*, 73.
8. Perkins, *With Justice for All*, 158.
9. Perkins, *Beyond Charity*, 97.
10. Perkins, *Beyond Charity*, 11.
11. Perkins tells the story of his early life in *Let Justice Roll Down* (Ventura, Calif.: Regal Books, 1976).
12. Perkins, *Beyond Charity*, 12.
13. Perkins, *Let Justice Roll Down*, 79.
14. Perkins, *With Justice for All*, 99.
15. Perkins, *With Justice for All*, 100–102.
16. Quoted by Margaret Smith in a profile of Perkins in *For a Change* (December 1988).
17. Perkins, *Beyond Charity*, 77.
18. Quoted in Perkins, *Beyond Charity*, 152.
19. Perkins, *With Justice for All*.
20. Perkins, *Beyond Charity*, 14–15.
21. Perkins, *Beyond Charity*.
22. UNDP, *Human Development Report, 1994* (New York/Oxford: Oxford University Press, 1994).
23. Perkins, *Beyond Charity*, 105–6.
24. Perkins, *Beyond Charity*.
25. Perkins, *Beyond Charity*, 88.

CHAPTER 12

Creative Connections in Pasadena

T he modern city is a vast web of structures, people, and needs. Herbert Girardet describes it as "the single most complex product of the human mind."[1] The problems interlock; urban violence, for instance, raises issues of policing, education, health (because of the role of alcohol and drugs), living conditions, and employment. But the responses tend to be sectoral, particularly in the social field. As needs multiply, agencies mushroom and compete for scarce resources.

John Perkins's city, Pasadena, California, has a population of 128,000,[2] and there are 225 human services agencies set up to meet their needs.[3] Over the last decade, there has been a bold church-based initiative to bring these agencies together to forge common strategies—particularly in the fields of child health and substance abuse.

Most Americans associate Pasadena with the annual New Year's Rose Parade and Rose Bowl football game and the California Institute of Technology. The city was once a dormitory for the bankers and industrialists of Los Angeles, eight miles away by freeway, and a winter home for wealthy easterners. In the last half century, it has undergone a demographic shift. Once predominantly monochrome and affluent, the city is now multicultural, with large pockets of poverty.

Over a quarter of Pasadena's population is Hispanic; nearly a fifth of the inhabitants are African American, and a tenth belong to Asian or other minority groups. Half the students in Pasadena's public school system come from low-income families;

over two-fifths qualify for free lunches; and a quarter find it difficult to communicate in English.⁴ Unemployment, homelessness, hunger, substance abuse, and violence destroy the lives of thousands of the city's inhabitants.

"There is no absence of agencies of goodwill," says Donald Miller, associate professor of social ethics at the University of Southern California. "But people from parallel agencies or groups often do not know each other, or else never get together to think more broadly about how their individual efforts might be combined to have a more strategic impact in the city."⁵ It was in an attempt to address this need that the church he attends launched the Office for Creative Connections.

All Saints Episcopal Church stands opposite city hall in downtown Pasadena. Since the early 1970s, when Pasadena first began to wake up to its changing reality, the church has been involved in social issues. "God has called us to do more than sing the songs on Sunday mornings," says its rector, George Regas.⁶

By the time of its centennial in 1983, All Saints had gathered some experience in acting as a catalyst in the community. In 1978, as concern about unemployment levels grew, it commissioned one of its members, John Wood, to look into the possibility of setting up a skills center to train people for entry-level jobs. Wood, then director of development for the Braille Institute, was no expert on skills training, so he embarked on eight months of consultation and interviews with all those concerned.

As a result, the superintendent of schools set up a task force made up of representatives of the school board, the community college, city government, and different communities. Under Wood's chairmanship, they met once or twice a week at 7:30 A.M. for four and a half months and came up with a proposal for a tripartite venture: the school board would provide the premises, Pasadena City College would provide administrative and teaching staff, and the city would act as a channel for funding and help with job placements.

The skills center opened in September 1980 with 1,200 students. By 1983, it was giving free training to 3,500 people a year, and two-thirds of them were going straight into jobs. Subjects included basic reading and writing, English as a second language, training for supermarket cashiers, electronics assembly, and a whole range of vocational skills. Today it trains up to 6,000 students a year.

The collaboration among school board, community college, and city government was unique in California's experience; so was the wide range of community members involved in the task force. "Representative and able those task force members were," John Wood told Basil Entwistle, who wrote a book about Pasadena's experience. "Of one mind they were not. As I look back now, I realize how essential it was to take the time to 'hear' each other during those weeks, and to learn from one another. We never took a vote. On every issue we were, at the end, of one mind."[7]

This was no small achievement. "The three governing units each had their turf to protect," says Walter Shatford, a trustee of Pasadena City College. "There had long been tension between the groups. To bring such competing factions together and get them to cooperate was no small enterprise."[8] Nico Rodriguez, then staff attorney for a Hispanic mutual assistance organization, found himself sitting across the table from people whose policies he had volubly opposed. "The fact that we came out of it with something everybody bought into and approved of—well, the unanimity of the task force was a miracle," he says.[9]

John Wood's role in the process was to float the idea in the community, gather a wide range of inputs, bring all the different interest groups together on neutral ground, and act as chairman. He was known to have no ax to grind, and he had a talent for bringing out the best in other people. It was a pattern that others at All Saints were to develop to good effect over the next decade.

In 1983, All Saints celebrated its centennial. As a gift to the city, the church asked Denise Wood—wife of John and recently retired dean of students at Marlborough School in Los Angeles—to survey the quality of life in Pasadena. She read all the research available, but, like her husband, she also decided to talk to people one-on-one. As one interview led to another over the next seven months, she met for breakfast once a week with Donald Miller and two other church members to review progress and map out strategy.

"One hundred and four interviews later I was not the same person I had been before the process began," she says. "The panorama of individuals' stories had taught me much of what others suffered, what they wanted as the basics of life, carried as painful memories, feared for their children. I recognized also that the people being listened to were being affected. What they had to say was held by someone else and by the church I represented as being important. They were being nurtured." She also found that through her interviews she was able to provide an informal link between people who shared similar concerns but did not know one another.

Wood's report, *Experiencing Pasadena—The Needs, Promises and Tasks of an American City,* revealed a city in pain. It made two recommendations: Pasadena must resist being polarized between the rich and the poor, and the well-being of its children should be everyone's concern. It also suggested that the church set up an office to continue the research and to provide "creative connections" between those working to improve things in the city.

The Office for Creative Connections (OCC) opened in May 1984, housed and funded by All Saints, with Denise Wood as its director. It started out by hosting roundtable meetings on children's issues: sexual and physical abuse, parenting skills, and early childhood development. The occasions included supper as well as discussion, so participants had a chance to get to know one another socially as well as professionally.

Early initiatives included a series of pilot summer youth employment programs (SYEPs), which provided both counseling and interesting work. "If you give a kid a job picking up cans, sure he has a job, but he gets a message about what you think of him," explains Denise Wood. As a result, the city now includes a counseling component in its SYEPs. The OCC also took up the issue of Pasadena's 8,000 latchkey kids, who often went home

P. Carr

*John and Denise Wood: tapping resources that
are usually covered up*

from school through gang territory to let themselves into empty
homes. Wood and her associate, Lorna Miller, joined with colleagues in the community to convince Pasadena's schools to keep
their doors open twelve hours a day so that parents could deliver
and collect their children before and after work.

In July 1985, the OCC received a grant from a Los Angeles
organization to "enhance and improve cooperation and communication between agencies serving youth at risk." The grant led
to three "listening" projects. Wood embarked on a study of teen-
age pregnancy, drugs, alcohol, and gangs and published her second report, *Growing Up in Pasadena: What Are Our Children
Telling Us?* in June 1986, during Pasadena's own centenary year.

In 1987, the centennial committee set up a city Commission on Children and Youth, with Denise Wood as its first chair, to speak up about children's issues to the city council.

Meanwhile, the OCC had commissioned Francisca Neumann to undertake a study of the resources available to confront substance abuse in Pasadena, and Lorna Miller to look into the accessibility of health services for children.

With 5.5 million serious addicts and, in 1991, 26 million casual drug users, the United States has the highest rates of drug abuse among industrialized countries. With the arrival of the crack epidemic in the mid-1980s, drug-related crime exploded. By the 1990s, over half of those arrested in large American cities tested positive for crack and cocaine; every year, 100,000 "crack babies" were born, damaged by their mothers' drug abuse. Drug abuse costs the nation an estimated $60 billion a year in terms of health care and lost productivity. Meanwhile, the cost of alcohol abuse runs to over $100 billion a year. The country has 18 million alcoholics.[10]

Both problems are particularly acute in southern California. By 1985, according to the *Los Angeles Times*, the area was "the world's largest retail market for cocaine."[11] And when the riots broke out in South Central Los Angeles in 1992, the neighborhood had more liquor stores than thirteen entire states.[12]

Eight miles away, in Pasadena and neighboring Altadena, substance abuse was also spiraling. In 1987, a group drawn together by the OCC commissioned Francisca Neumann, herself a recovering alcoholic, to conduct a survey into drug and alcohol abuse in the two communities. She quickly realized that the problems could not be tackled in isolation. "When you have a problem like violence, there is a lot of alcohol- and drug-related fueling of the fire," she says. "Under that you have the quality of life and inequities of society. The problems reach all the way down to soul-sickness within. It's not just a problem of law enforcement or education."

If the problems were to be addressed, it was clear that concerned groups would need to work together. In April 1988, the

OCC launched a community partnership to fight substance abuse, Day One. It aimed to overcome the bureaucratic wrangling that had hampered earlier campaigns. Neumann, who became its executive director, describes the twenty-five-agency coalition as "a circle of wagons."

Day One's motto is "Take charge of your life; take care of your community." It acts as a catalyst and a link rather than creating programs itself. For instance, it brought the heads of local treatment centers together and pointed out that many who needed inpatient treatment could not afford it because they had no health insurance. Fourteen free beds were pledged. On another occasion, Myrtle Glenn, a counselor in northwest Pasadena, came to Day One concerned about pregnant drug users who could not get treatment because existing centers would not accommodate their children. Neumann helped persuade the Junior League to support a new center with facilities for mothers and children.

The coalition focuses on prevention. Members have set up "sober centers" (drug- and alcohol-free recreation areas), stopped the selling of single cans of cold beer to discourage drinking in public places, and set up summer activities and training and awareness programs for schools and businesses. They also issue a manual on prevention and treatment resources in the area. A federal grant has enabled Day One to reach out to people at risk through a "small but highly visible staff of mostly young people who are out on the streets and in the parks and meeting rooms."[13]

According to Pasadena's chief of police, Jerry Oliver, Day One's work gave the city the courage to ban the sale of alcohol during the 1994 World Cup soccer games at the Rose Bowl. In a city packed with soccer fans from all over the world, there were only a handful of alcohol-related arrests.

Day One's achievement has been twofold, according to Neumann. First, it has made Pasadena and Altadena aware of the role of alcohol and drugs in undermining the quality of life and health. "This is not a popular topic," she says. "People do not like to look at problem areas that might come back at them. They prefer to target poor communities, which they can fence off."

Second, it has succeeded in getting people to work together. "When two or more are gathered together, you lose a bit of yourself but get a bigger result." The collaborative approach to substance abuse has taken off all over the United States in recent years, with some 3,000 coalitions in existence. Day One was one of the first, though not the only model.

"In the war against drugs . . . the dumbest way for society to spend money is, of course, at the end of the equation," wrote Pasadena's *Star-News* on Febuary 10, 1991. It continued:

> That's the policing end, the social worker end, the emergency hospital end, the divorce court end, the in-patient detoxification program end. Everything down there is costly, in human and economic terms.
>
> Up front is where Day One works. . . . It's about empowerment, about taking charge and care rather than, collectively, letting our friends and neighbors and families and selves throw it away.

One in three children attending public school in Pasadena has no health insurance,[14] in a country where most medical care is private. If one of these children fell sick five years ago, the parents had only two options: to take the child to the city's only low-cost walk-in clinic, which opened once a week for two hours, or to go to a hospital emergency room at a prohibitive cost. Today, thanks to the Young and Healthy program, every uninsured low-income schoolchild in Pasadena has access to free care.

True to OCC form, Young and Healthy was born out of the listening process. In 1987, Lorna Miller, then associate director of OCC, embarked on an investigation of the health of Pasadena's children. The daughter of refugees of the Armenian genocide of 1915, she had spent fifteen years interviewing survivors of the massacre and had considerable experience in listening. She published a report in June 1988 and called together interested parties for a series of working lunches, which gave birth to the Health Coalition for Children and Youth. By May 1989, it had twenty-four members and a slogan: "It is the right of every child to have access to quality health care."

Under the chairmanship of Donald Thomas, an emergency-room physician at Pasadena's largest hospital, the coalition aimed

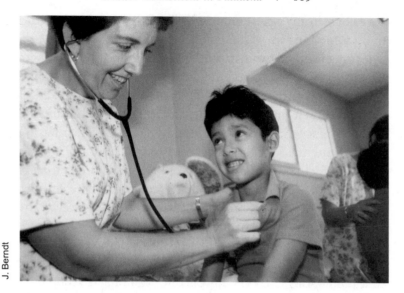

An uninsured child receives free healthcare thanks to Pasadena's Young and Healthy program

to widen the doorway of each doctor's office so that needy children could squeeze through. He set about persuading doctors to offer one or two free appointments per month. The program started out with eighteen doctors. By 1995, it had a network of 220 doctors; dentists; eye, foot, and mental health specialists; nurses; and therapists. A network of pharmacies offers free prescriptions, and a laboratory provides free tests.

This means that any child without health insurance who goes to the school nurse with a problem that needs attention can be referred, through the Young and Healthy office, to a doctor who will provide service free of charge. Volunteers provide backup services—ferrying children to appointments, helping with translation, and following through with children and parents. The scheme embraces Pasadena's thirty-two public elementary, middle, and high schools, with a total of some 22,000 children.

The program is unique, according to Philip Porter, director of Healthy Children, a community health program linked to Harvard's Division of Health Policy Research and Education.

"I've not seen any other community like Pasadena come together to do something for children," he told the *Los Angeles Times*.[15] The paper featured two sisters, Selina and Norma Martinez, aged six and seven, who had received treatment through the scheme. Their parents earned some $200 a week, paid rent of $275 a month for their one-room home, and lacked health insurance.

In its first year, Young and Healthy made 227 referrals for medical care for 120 children. In its fourth year, 1993–94, it helped 900 children and young people by providing a total of 2,543 "units of service." By catching problems before children become seriously ill, the program has cut school absenteeism and hospital admissions. Apart from its two managers, who are paid through foundation grants, the program is staffed completely by volunteers. Its office is provided, rent free, by the board of education. Other cities in California are beginning to set up similar schemes.

Each city is unique and has to find its own solutions. What Pasadena's experience has to offer is a process through which these solutions can be sought. Denise Wood formulates the process in four stages:

1. Listen to the people of the community one by one and to its public bodies to gain a living picture of its needs, its strengths, and its possibilities.
2. Discern the meaning of what has been heard and the imperatives of what must be addressed.
3. Picture the community back to itself—not name-calling, not blaming, but not watering down the truth either— and speak with a moral voice to the whole community.
4. Connect citizens around common concerns and create coalitions and structures to carry out what needs to be done.

During the first two stages of the process, she says, a spiritual dynamic is at work. The one-on-one interviews (the OCC never mails a questionnaire) provide an opportunity to get beyond knee-jerk reactions and lists of statistics to reach deeper insights. "When people come to a hearing, they're likely to posture a little and defend their point of view," Wood says. "One-on-one in their own setting, they're more likely to express things in a more thoughtful way." The method is time-consuming, but "when you get to the policy stage, you can go much faster," because trust has been built at the interview stage.

"For those doing the listening, there is a step of reflecting, of discerning," says Wood. It has two components: reflecting on what has been heard, and reflecting on what it has meant to the listener to become part of another person's story. "This is where the moral imperatives become clear and where the decision is made to commit to them and take consequent action." Her weekly meetings with her three colleagues at All Saints helped her digest what she had been told, recharge her batteries, and decide how to proceed.

Out of these two steps issue the more tangible steps: the report on what has been heard, and the connecting of people for action. For Fran Neumann, OCC's uniqueness rests in the latter: "the ability and willingness to connect, to move it out, not just to bring it here and keep it." It is the difference between saying "Oh boy, this is a wonderful person for my committee!" and saying "Oh boy, this is a wonderful person; who would find her most helpful?" Neumann frequently sends people on from Day One to other agencies, just as she passes on information about grant opportunities. The aim is to get the job done, not to build her own empire. She relishes the point at which the initiatives inspired by Day One spin out of her control and become institutions in their own right.

Behind the process lies a mind-set "of drawing the best out of people, of choosing coalition and trust rather than confrontation, and of thinking for the community as a whole," says Denise Wood. When she spoke about the OCC in Chicago recently, a veteran community activist contrasted her approach with the more confrontational methods of social campaigner Saul Alinsky. "What Saul Alinsky was talking about was fission," he said. "What you are talking about is fusion."

The Woods say that their approach was influenced by twenty-five years spent working overseas with an international organization concerned with human development. "Living in many different countries with different cultures, we learned that everyone matters and that you have to leave your stereotypes at the door," says Denise. She rarely talks about her faith, which she found as a student at Vassar, but sees it as fundamental. "It gets you up in the morning, prevents burnout, teaches you to listen to other people, to believe that things will happen. I used to play a lot of touch football. My faith gives me the courage to make a forward pass and believe that someone up ahead will catch it."[16]

For Francisca Neumann, a Unitarian, belief is a source of hope and of passion: "People ask me why I care about these children. I say, because they are *mine*. It hurts me when I see kids who are likely to become statistics. And if I see an old man peeing on the street, I think, that's somebody's child out there."

In 1990, the Woods moved to Pennsylvania, and Lorna Miller took over as director of the OCC. The Woods are now involved in a listening process in their new hometown of Kennett Square, a rural community with a significant Mexican and Puerto Rican population. "You have to work differently in a small community, where everyone knows what everyone else had for breakfast," explains Denise. "You move quietly. But we are seeing a group of rugged individualists beginning to say 'we.'" The Woods are also involved in helping a similar initiative get started in Bermuda.

In Chicago, priest and banker Bliss Williams Browne has come up with a similar approach to the OCC's. Imagine Chicago is using twenty pairs of interviewers to uncover people's dreams of what Chicago could be. Each pair teams up a young adult from some of the city's toughest housing projects with an older person. "They are ploughing the same ground and discovering many of the same things," observes Denise Wood. "We are becoming staunch collaborators."

Meanwhile, All Saints in Pasadena is involved in a new issue: teen violence. Its rector convened the Committee for a Nonviolent City in 1993 after three teenagers on their way home from a Halloween party were killed by gang members. The initiative has two prongs: to get the guns out of people's hands, and to deal with the root causes. The OCC is coordinating research on the latter. As I write, it is still in the listening phase, with some twenty volunteers gathering information on what facilities exist for young people in Pasadena when they are not in school.

The OCC celebrated its tenth anniversary in May 1994. Unlike some of the other examples in this book, it works on the level of the city macrocosm as well as the neighborhood microcosm and invests time in listening to professional caregivers and officials as well as people at the grassroots. The OCC offers a model of how a nonspecialist, spiritually motivated group can act as a catalyst by providing a nonpartisan ear for a city's hope and pain, a neutral ground on which different interest groups and specialists can meet, and the persistence to make things happen.

"One of the essentials is raising the hope factor," Denise Wood told a conference of civic leaders in Richmond, Virginia, in 1991. "You can diagnose a problem so much that you can run yourself into the ground. Our discovery is, there's a spark in everybody, and if you can create a plan and a climate and a trust, and express well enough a real need, you tap resources that are usually covered up."

Notes

This chapter is drawn from the sources cited below and from interviews and correspondence with Denise Wood and interviews with Francisca Neumann and Lorna Miller. See also Basil Entwistle's article in *For a Change* (February/March 1995).

1. Herbert Girardet, *The Gaia Atlas of Cities* (London: Gaia Books, 1992), 19.
2. Margaret Smith, "Pasadena's Long-Distance Runners," *For a Change*, November 1987.
3. Basil Entwistle, *Making Cities Work* (Pasadena: Hope Publishing House, 1992).
4. *Young and Healthy in Pasadena*, published by Healthy Children, a nationwide program administered at Harvard University's Division of Health Policy Research and Education.

5. Donald E. Miller, foreword to *Making Cities Work* by Basil Entwistle, xiii.
6. Quoted in *Young and Healthy in Pasadena,* 5.
7. Entwistle, *Making Cities Work,* 13.
8. Entwistle, *Making Cities Work,* 17–18.
9. Entwistle, *Making Cities Work,* 15–16.
10. Mathea Falco, *The Making of a Drug-Free America: Programs That Work* (New York: Times Books, 1991).
11. Quoted in Entwistle, *Making Cities Work.*
12. *U.S. News & World Report,* May 31, 1993.
13. *Pasadena Star-News,* April 27, 1993.
14. *Young and Healthy in Pasadena.*
15. *Los Angeles Times,* February 18, 1993.
16. Quoted in Smith, "Pasadena's Long-Distance Runners."

CHAPTER 13

Long-Distance Runners

The congregation of All Saints in Pasadena, California and the villagers of Ralegan Siddhi, India, could hardly be farther apart in their standards of living, daily rounds, culture, and expectations. What they have in common is that they are people of faith—though they express this in different ways—and that this has spurred them into action.

From Jamshedpur, India, to Atlanta, Georgia, from the favelas of Rio de Janeiro to the *kohanga* of New Zealand, from the village of Walkerswood to inner-city London, grassroots communities have found that spiritual experience is a resource in community development. It can empower the powerless and give community leaders the strength to persevere through the inevitable ups and downs—to be, in the words of Denise Wood of Pasadena, "long-distance runners."

The resurrection of Ralegan Siddhi began in the village temple. The work of Sarvodaya in Sri Lanka, of John Perkins in the southern United States, of Kohanga Reo in New Zealand, and of Telco's Human Relations at Work program in Jamshedpur drew on the spiritual heritage of those involved. They demonstrate what can be achieved by working with people's beliefs rather than against them. In ancient Sri Lanka, temples were built out of the earth excavated when irrigation canals and tanks (reservoirs) were dug.[1] This partnership of temple and tank offers a metaphor for an approach in which spiritual and material development go hand in hand.

171

"Changing a life and changing a community is ultimately a spiritual issue," maintains John Perkins.[2] For many of the people in this book, material development is a by-product, not an end in itself. Some would go even further: "Development involves more than material growth and includes the progress of all from ignorance of reality to enlightenment," states Sarvodaya. "Material well-being is no more than the vehicle necessary for spiritual awakening."[3]

This longer view is one of the strengths of faith-driven community leaders. Communities and people are volatile, and the path of progress is paved with mistakes and disappointments. People whose perspective extends into eternity have more staying power than those whose source of self-worth is short-term success. Faced with the possible collapse of the Bridge Park center in London, Errol Williams could talk of the difference in his feelings when he looked at the situation "from God's perspective." He maintained that in the context of eternity, what the center had done for individuals was more important than its founders' reputations.

In the fifty-plus years since it set out on the road of self-help, the village of Walkerswood in Jamaica has had its share of conflict and reversals. Its leaders maintain that it is hard for those who "do not know" the Lord to cope with the ups and downs. It owes its continued progress to a hard core of people who draw their resilience from their faith and refuse to give up.

For most of the people in this book, there was a moment of decision, a Damascus Road encounter or an experience of calling from which there could be no turning back. For Anna Hazare, it was a brush with death; for Americo Martorelli, a conversation at a bus stop; for Lawrence Fearon, a vision in a city park; for John Perkins, an experience in a church. For the founders of Black Teens for Advancement, it was the realization at a basketball game that they could take their destiny into their own hands. For José Carlos de Souza in Nova Holanda and for Sunil Mukherji in Jamshedpur, the door to community action opened as they began to fight back from alcohol dependence. The experience of moral change—of liberation from addiction, reconciliation with an enemy, new relations in the family—can be profoundly empowering.

There are, of course, pitfalls for faith-driven initiatives, as for all others. The belief that God is on one's side, reinforced by the conviction that prayer has been answered, can engender a lack of realism about the importance of human agencies and accountability. A strong bond of belief can lead to exclusiveness and sometimes rigidity. A project may collapse when a strong, charismatic leader moves on or becomes sidetracked. People may take advantage of others' high ideals—or feel that their own goodwill is being exploited. Spiritual motivation cannot be taken for granted; it has to be continually renewed from within. And the conflicts that break out between believers can be among the bloodiest.

The most sustainable initiatives are those whose animators retain the flexibility to learn from experience and to adapt to new circumstances. This has been a strength of Walkerswood. Over a period of fifty years, trends and aspirations change. For people of spiritual conviction, there will always be a tension between following one's own vision and accepting that other people's agendas are also valid.

These requirements apply to professionals as well as to grass-roots workers, to the secularly minded as well as to the spiritual. "One of the biggest problems in the NGO [nongovernmental organization] movement is that they do not understand that they cannot determine the way people think and behave," says development networker and journalist Donatus da Silva. "You can enable a person to move from his or her life of fate and realize his or her destiny. But what that destiny is, is between him or her and God."

"One of my own unscientific conclusions is that half of what happens in a community is because people want to be noticed, to know that they are cared for," says Selena Tapper, Caribbean field officer for Canadian Universities Service Overseas (CUSO). "If people learn respect for themselves and for others and discover that they can think, then even if this project doesn't work, the next may."

The motivation of the development worker is crucial, she believes. "Is it just a job? Or a way of lording it over people who are less well off than I am? Of saying, it's fine for you to become self-sufficient and confident as long as you understand that your position is subservient to mine? Or is it to engage in a struggle which is also part of changing me? Unless the development worker or helper is also prepared to change, we won't change systems of injustice."

"To an extraordinary degree, we, development professionals, abstain from looking at ourselves," wrote development analyst Robert Chambers.

> Yet who we are, where we go, how we behave, what we are shown and see, how we learn, are deceived, and deceive ourselves, the concepts we use, the language we speak, what we believe, and above all what we do and do not do—these so obviously affect all other aspects of development and development policy. . . . As a matter not of evangelism, but of analytical rigor, it would seem that it is we the professionals, the powerful and the influential . . . who have to reconstruct our realities, to change as people, and to enable and empower others to change, if the new paradigm of development is to prevail.[4]

Institutional religious responses to suffering have not always been benign. Christian denominations have been particularly prone to narrowness and soul-snatching. The Irish still talk of Catholics who "took the soup" during the famine of the 1840s, succumbing to pressure to become Protestants in exchange for food. As recently as 1993, victims of the Maharashtra earthquake found themselves assailed by Christian tracts urging them to convert.[5] Such practices are wholly unethical.

When religious organizations see their role as one of service rather than proselytization and refuse to play favorites, their independence is their strength. The Mel Nathan Institute, founded in a middle-class church in a deprived community in Kingston, Jamaica, runs educational and business development programs. It makes a point of not asking about people's politics or religion.

"In a Third World situation you find that when development is initiated by government, it is often tainted by politics," says its executive director of financial services, Anserd C. Williams. "A lot of programs started by the state get scrapped when a new party comes into power. You need agencies like the church to get involved and see that impartiality prevails. We're not looking for a second term of office."

In Pasadena, All Saints Church has made a virtue of its amateur status, providing a neutral ground on which social welfare professionals can meet and find a common cause. And in Bradford, Muslims, Hindus, Sikhs, and Christians have been working together to break down the barriers between their city's faith communities rather than retreating behind the barricades or fanning the fires.

The experiences of the people in this book show that no one is helpless. The springs of action and initiative, of hope and perseverance, lie within. Effective social change can start with personal change: in fact, it will be more sustainable if it does. Far from being an opiate, religion can be the source of liberation, empowerment, and community development.

Notes

Unless otherwise stated, quotations come from my own interviews.

1. Joanna Macy, *Dharma and Development: Religion as Resource in the Sarvodaya Self-Help Movement*, rev. ed. (West Hartford, Conn.: Kumarian Press, 1985).
2. John M. Perkins, *Beyond Charity* (Grand Rapids, Mich.: Baker Books, 1993), 80.
3. Paper presented by Sarvodaya to a Commonwealth-sponsored Poverty Alleviation Consultation, Colombo, October 1991.
4. Robert Chambers, "Poverty and Livelihoods: Whose Reality Counts?" (overview paper for the UNDP Stockholm Roundtable on Global Change, July 1994).
5. Alan Nichols, "Ethical Issues in Evangelism and Justice Among the Poor," *Evangelical Review of Theology*, April 1994.

Index

176